ESTE LIBRO MUY IMPORTANTE
QUE ES "LA BIBLIA" ES UN
REGALO DE TIA PATY PARA
ELIZABETH, JOCELYN Y MICHAEL
ESPERANDO LES SIRVA COMO GUIA
PARA LOS TIEMPOS QUE ESTAN
POR VENIR.... QUE ELIZABETH
COMO HERMANA MAYOR SEA
EJEMPLO DE AMOR, TOLERANCIA
Y RESPETO PARA CON SUS
PEQUEÑOS HERMANOS QUE LA
AMAN POR LO QUE ELLA
SIGNIFICA PARA ELLOS

NOV - 13 - 2010.

TIA PATY

TIA PATY

To

ELIZABETH

From

NOV - 13 - 2010

Date

Standard
BIBLE
STORYBOOK

Retold by Carolyn Larsen

Standard®
PUBLISHING

Cincinnati, Ohio

Published by Standard Publishing, Cincinnati, Ohio

www.standardpub.com

Printed in: Malaysia

Project editors: Elaina Meyers and Dawn A. Medill

Cover design: Diane Bay

Illustrations from Standard Publishing's Classic Bible Art Collection

Published in association with Educational Publishing Concepts

ISBN 978-0-7847-2360-9

Library of Congress Cataloging-in-Publication Data

Larsen, Carolyn, 1950-
 Standard bible storybook / retold by Carolyn Larsen.
   p. cm.
 ISBN 978-0-7847-2360-9 (casebound)
 1. Bible stories, English. I. Title.
 BS551.3.L376 2009
 220.9'505--dc22

                         2009026796

14 13 12 11 10 09   1 2 3 4 5 6 7 8 9

To Jude and Brody . . .

I pray that these precious stories teach you much about our living, loving God.

I pray that you come to know Him early and enjoy learning about Him and serving Him all your lives.

Love you!

CONTENTS
The Old Testament

The Story of Isaac

Jacob's Story

The Life of Joseph

The Story of Moses

The First King of Israel

David Is King

The Reign of Solomon

Trouble for Israel

Stories of Elisha

Judah's Last Days

Daniel and His Friends

The Story of Queen Esther

God's People Return

The Story of Jonah

The New Testament

He Came Before

Jesus Is Born

Jesus Growing Up

The Ministry of John

Preparation for Ministry

Jesus' Ministry Begins

Jesus' Teachings

Jesus Teaches by Telling Stories

Jesus Teaches by Healing

Jesus Teaches by Doing Miracles

A Look at Glory

The Last Days

The Young Church

INTRODUCTION

T he Bible is an amazing book! It is the incredibly detailed story of God's work among His people. As it is read from beginning to end, the reader sees God's plan unfold. His spectacular work at Creation is finished with the creation of man and woman, made in God's own image. Then begins the journey of humans knowing, loving, and serving God. It's a struggle sometimes and the Bible tells us the good parts and the difficult parts.

This Bible storybook shows how the familiar stories and people of the Bible are connected. The Bible is not 66 sections that have nothing to do with each other. Each book and each story builds on one another to give a complete picture of God's amazing love and grace. He desires a relationship with each human on this earth and He does everything He can to make that possible. The stories of Old Testament peoples' obedience and failures lead right to God's gift of Jesus' birth—the beginning of His plan to make a bridge from man's sin to God's Heaven. Jesus' life on Earth gives us

His teachings, stories, miracles, and examples of how to live with others and live for God. His death, though difficult to read about, leads right into the account of His resurrection and the gift of the Holy Spirit. Amazing! The rest of the Bible shows how God's people spread the message of His love. In the process they have written down His teachings and encouragement to help people continue to spread the Good News until Jesus returns—and He is coming back!

The classic artwork that illustrates these stories was commissioned by Standard Publishing. Between 1908 and 1948 more than 800 oil paintings, depicting all the major events of the Bible, were created by several painters from European art schools. Each picture gives an understanding of the setting and culture of the biblical story. Therefore, each picture is a lesson in history as well as an illustration of the story.

All those involved in creating this book pray that it will be God's tool in drawing the readers closer to Him; giving them a more complete picture of the thread of God's work throughout history and His constant love and grace toward people. Hopefully, it will be one more stepping stone for children to progress from reading children's Bible storybooks to the actual "grown-up" Word of God.

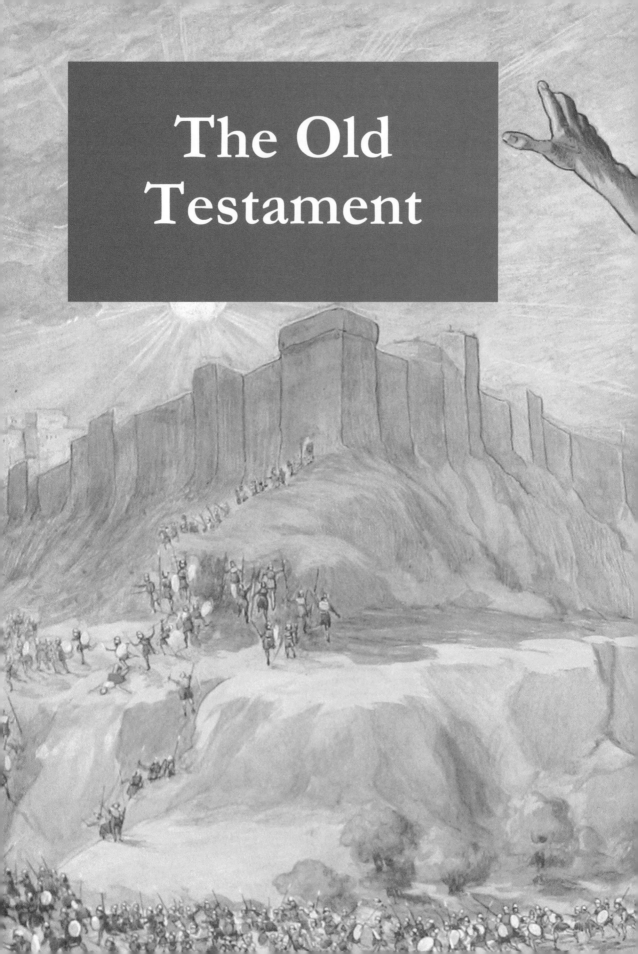

The Old Testament

CREATION

The miracle of creation showed God's amazing power and creativity. It also showed how much He cares for mankind. He created a beautiful world for us to enjoy, whether you love mountains, oceans, or deserts. He made tiny hummingbirds and gigantic killer whales. He made delicate yellow flowers and huge redwood trees. God thought of everything and He made something for everyone to enjoy . . . creation shows God's love!

The Creation *Genesis 1:1-25*

Before there were people on Earth . . . before there were animals on Earth . . . before there was a sun or a moon . . . before there was even an earth, there was only emptiness, darkness, and silence. Then God spoke four simple words, "Let there be light," and the miracle of creation began. The earth and everything in it was made by God. He did it all in six days.

God began Day One of creation by making light and darkness. He separated

the light and dark from each other. He called the light, *day* and the darkness *night*.

Day Two of creation God created waters above the earth—in the heavens, and water on Earth itself. Then He created the sky and put it between the waters of Heaven and Earth.

On Day Three, God moved the waters on Earth together and separated them from the dry land. He called the waters *seas* and the dry ground *land*. He filled the land with plants and trees that grow fruits with seeds. His plan was that the seeds would drop to the ground and make new plants. That way the plants would keep growing more plants and fill the earth with flowers, bushes, and trees.

On Day Four, God put a light in the night-time sky. This light is the moon. He also put stars in the night sky. God put a brighter light in the day-time sky. This light is the sun.

Day Five saw the creation of fish and other life in the seas. From the tiniest little seahorse to the mammoth blue whale, God filled the waters with life. Day Five is also the day that God made birds that fly through the sky. These sea creatures and sky creatures have babies so there will always be life in the seas and in the sky.

On Day Six God made all kinds of animals that live on the earth. He made insects like mosquitoes and caterpillars. He made small animals such as squirrels and kittens. He made large animals such as elephants and giraffes. He made farm animals like cows and goats. God told all the animals to have babies so that the earth would always be filled with animals.

God looked at everything He had made. He was very happy with all of creation. He had made seas and dry land. He had filled the seas with things that swim and He had filled the land with animals and plants. He had made the sun and the moon. But God wasn't finished yet. There was one more special creation on Day Six. This one is God's masterpiece!

God Makes People *Genesis 1:26–2:3*

For six days God was busy creating things. He made the whole earth and everything in it. Each of His creations was amazing. But on the sixth day, God made His most incredible creation. He made the first man using just the dust of the earth. Adam was made in God's own image. That means that people could think, make choices, talk, and care about things just as God

does. "Adam," God said, "I want you to give names to each of the animals I have created." Adam named them all, "That is a butterfly. This one I will call hippopotamus." But, when the naming was finished, Adam was lonely. He had no other human to be friends with; no one to talk with. God saw that Adam was lonely, so He made Adam fall asleep. While Adam was sleeping, God took a rib from his side. God used that rib to form another human. This human was different from Adam though. She was a woman. She was called "Eve."

Adam and Eve were the first people on Earth. God told them to have babies and fill the earth with more people. He trusted them to govern the earth and take care of it. God made a beautiful garden in Eden for Adam and Eve to live in. "I have given you plants to eat and trees that grow fruit to enjoy. I also made plants for the animals to eat," God said. When God was finished with all this, the sixth day ended. God looked at everything He had made. It was all good. God was happy with everything. So, on the next day, the seventh day, God rested.

Sin Enters the World *Genesis 2:8–3:24*

God put wonderful plants in the Garden of Eden that grew sweet berries and other delicious fruit for Adam and Eve to eat. Four rivers supplied water for them to drink. Adam and Eve had everything they needed in the Garden of Eden. God gave them important work to do. Their job was to care for the garden and rule over the animals that lived there. God gave Adam

and Eve one simple rule to obey. He said, "You can eat fruit from any of the trees in the garden. They are all here for you to enjoy. But you must not eat fruit from the tree in the center of the garden. If you eat from the Tree of Knowledge of Good and Evil, you will die."

The serpent was the sneakiest of all the creatures God made. One day he crept up to Eve and asked, "Did God really say that you can't eat *any* of the fruit in the garden?"

"Of course not," Eve replied. "We can eat whatever we want except for the fruit of the tree in the center of the garden. If we eat that fruit, we will die."

"Oh, come on," the serpent said. "You won't really die. If you eat that fruit you will just become more like God. You will actually know the difference between good and evil."

The serpent kept tempting Eve to try the fruit and it looked so juicy and delicious that finally she grabbed a piece and took a bite. It was just as tasty as it looked so Eve gave Adam some of it too. Right at the moment they ate the fruit both Adam and Eve knew they were naked so they quickly tied some leaves together to make clothes.

Later than night God came to meet the man and the woman in the garden.

But Adam and Eve were ashamed because they had disobeyed God, so they hid from Him. When God asked Adam why he was hiding, Adam answered, "I was afraid because I am naked."

"Who told you that you are naked?" God asked. "Did you eat the fruit I commanded you not to eat?"

"I did. But Eve is the one who gave it to me," Adam answered.

"Yes, but the serpent tricked me into eating it," Eve said.

God was very sad that they had disobeyed Him, but He had to punish Adam and Eve. So God made Adam and Eve leave the beautiful Garden of Eden. He even stationed a flaming sword at the opening of the Garden so Adam and Eve could never go back inside.

Cain and Abel *Genesis 4:1-16*

After being sent out of the Garden of Eden, Adam and Eve had two sons. Cain was the oldest and when he grew up he became a farmer. Abel was his younger brother and he became a shepherd when he grew up. Adam and Eve taught their sons to give offerings to God. So, at harvest time, Cain brought an offering of grain he grew on his farm. He presented his

offering to God. Abel brought the Lord a gift of one of the best lambs from his best flock of sheep. The Lord accepted Abel's offering but He rejected Cain's offering. Cain became very angry.

"What are you angry about, Cain?" God asked. "Your offering will be accepted if you do what is right. If you do not do what is right and respond in the right way then watch out because sin is going to destroy you!"

Cain could not get over his anger. The more he thought about his offering being rejected the angrier he got. He became jealous that Abel's offering was accepted so his anger was directed at his brother. Cain came up with an evil plan. One afternoon he suggested, "Abel, let's go out to the field together." Abel went for a walk with his brother out to the field. While they were away from everyone else, Cain attacked his brother and killed him. He thought no one would know what he had done.

But later God asked Cain, "Where is your brother, Abel?"

"I don't know," Cain lied. "Do You expect me to keep track of him every minute?"

But God knew what Cain had done. "You killed your brother," God said. "His blood cries out to me from the ground where you left him. I must punish you for what you have done. This ground will no longer grow crops for you, no matter how hard you work," God said. "Also, I will make you leave this place you call home." For the rest of his life Cain would have no real place to call home.

"This punishment is too hard," Cain complained. "You are sending me away from my land and away from Your presence. Everyone who sees me will try to kill me!"

"No one will kill you," the Lord said. "I will severely punish anyone who does." Just to be sure, God put a mark on Cain to warn anyone who might try to hurt him. So Cain left God's presence and settled in another land.

Noah's Story

After Cain killed his brother, Adam and Eve had another son. They named him Seth. When Seth grew up, he had a son named Enosh. During his lifetime people began to pray to God. About seven generations later a man named Noah was born. By then many people had stopped praying to God. They stopped obeying God. In fact, they just didn't care about God at all. Of course, it made God sad because the people He had created no longer cared about Him. But Noah still cared about obeying God, and his story changed everything.

Noah Builds an Ark *Genesis 6:1-22*

Adam and Eve had children. Their children had children. Now, generations later, the population of Earth was growing very quickly. It seemed that the more people who lived on Earth, the more selfish and greedy people became. Of course, God noticed that people had become very self-centered. Each one thought only about himself and how things affected him. It made God sad to see how evil people had become. They were dishonest and they didn't care at all about living for God or pleasing Him. They even did things that hurt one another. You know that things must have gotten very bad because God began to feel sorry He had even made people. His heart was filled with sadness and pain. He knew that He had to do something to stop people's evil behavior. So God came up with a plan. It was a good plan but it would not be easy for His loving heart. He said, "I will wipe out all the people on Earth—everyone I have created. I will wipe animals and birds from the face of the earth too, because I am sorry I made them all." However, there was one man on Earth who pleased God. His name was Noah.

Noah obeyed God even though his friends and neighbors did not. God saw Noah's obedience. He saw that Noah taught his three sons, Shem, Ham, and Japheth, to obey God. So God said, "Noah, I'm tired of the violence and evil ways of my people. I have decided to destroy the people and the animals of Earth. I want to save you because you honor me. So build an ark, a big boat." God told Noah exactly how big to make this giant boat and exactly what kind of wood to use and how to build it. He gave him specific instructions. The ark would be 450 feet long, 75 feet wide, and 45 feet high! It would have one window all the way around and very near the top of the boat. It would have one giant door on one side.

God said to build three decks inside: one on the bottom, one in the middle, and one on top.

God planned to destroy the world and the people in it by sending a flood over all the earth. This flood would wipe everything God had made off the face of the earth. But Noah and his family would be safe inside the ark.

"I want you to bring inside the ark with you two of every kind of animal and bird that lives on Earth," God told Noah. God made a male and a female of each species of animal come to Noah. Monkeys, camels, rabbits, goats, eagles, sparrows—all the birds and animals that God had created went inside the ark and lived on the three decks Noah had built inside. "Bring food onto the ark for you and your family and for all the animals too," God said. Noah did everything that God told him to do.

The Rain Begins *Genesis 7:1–8:5*

Noah finished building the ark exactly as God told him to build it. It took Noah many years to build the ark, but he kept working. When it was finished and all the animals were safely inside, God said, "Noah, take your family and go inside the ark too." It was time for God's plan to go into action. God shut Noah, his family, and all the animals inside the ark and rain began to fall. Remember, there was a male and a female of every kind of animal in the ark along with Noah, his wife, their sons Shem, Ham, Japheth, and their sons' wives. Noah had stored lots of food for all the animals and for his family in the giant boat too. He didn't know how long they would be in the ark, but God knew.

Noah was 600 years old when it began to rain. It rained and rained. Rivers got so full that water began to spill over the banks. Giant puddles formed on the ground. Pretty soon the ground was completely covered with water. The people couldn't tell where the rivers or lakes had once been separated from the dry land. They may have been worried about when the rain was going to stop. God's plan continued and it kept right on raining. The floodwaters got deeper and deeper. Finally the water was as high as the tops of the trees. Inside the ark, Noah, his family, and all the animals were safe and dry. They could hear the rain falling outside. As the water got deeper and deeper, it lifted Noah's giant boat right off the ground and it began floating.

The rain kept falling steadily on the earth for 40 days and 40 nights. It didn't stop raining. Soon, even the tallest mountains were covered with 20 feet of water. The great ark floated higher and higher—as high as the top of the mountains. Still Noah and everyone in the ark was safe. But outside the ark things were not so good. Everything on the earth was destroyed. Every single person living on the earth died in the flood. All of the animals—birds, sheep, goats, cows, dogs—all of them drowned. Trees, plants, flowers, and bushes—everything was destroyed, just as God said they would be. No one was left on Earth except Noah and his family.

After 40 days and 40 nights the rain stopped falling. But the floodwaters were so deep that the ark kept floating and floating. The waters covered the earth for 150 days.

God remembered Noah and He sent a strong wind to start blowing across the earth. It began drying up the floodwaters. The water went down and down until finally the ark came to rest on the top of a mountain called Ararat. But the floodwaters were still too deep for Noah to let the animals out of the boat. Noah and his family had been living in the ark for about eight months but it still wasn't safe to come out. They couldn't live on the earth yet.

A Brand New Start *Genesis 8:6–9:17*

Noah's giant boat came to rest on the top of Mount Ararat when the floodwaters began going down. The water was still too deep for Noah and his family to come out so they waited 40 days. Then Noah sent a raven out. It flew back and forth, looking for a place to land. After a while Noah sent a dove out of the ark. It flew around and around but could not find

a place to land so it came back to the ark. Noah waited a week and then sent the dove out again. It came back to the ark again, but this time it had an olive leaf in its beak! The water was going down! Noah sent the dove out once more a week later. This time it didn't even come back! It was still a couple of months later before God finally said, "Come out of the ark, Noah. Bring out your family and all the animals. It's time for the animals and birds to have babies and fill the earth with life once again." So Noah and his family came out of the ark and saw the brand new world that was left after the flood. The fresh air smelled good. The sunshine felt good. But there were no other people or animals on Earth. They had all died in the flood. The only people and animals now were the ones who had been inside the ark.

The first thing Noah did was build an altar and give a sacrifice to God. He thanked God for keeping him and his family safe from the flood. His whole family thanked God too. God was pleased with the sacrifice and He said, "I will never curse the ground again. Even though man is evil, I will not destroy the earth and all its creatures again. As long as the earth is here, there will be summer and winter and day and night."

"I bless you and your sons, Noah. I want you and your sons to have more children so the earth will be populated again. You will rule over the animals and I give you all the plants. I give you everything," God said.

Then God made a promise to Noah and his sons. "Never again will I cut off all life from the earth by a great flood. There will never again be a flood as big as this one. I promise," God said. "I will put a sign in the sky as a reminder of my promise. Each time I see this sign I will remember my promise to you." The sign God put in the sky was the very first rainbow! Noah knew that the rainbow was a reminder of God's promise with all the creatures on Earth. Noah and his family were ready for a brand new start.

THE TOWER OF BABEL

Noah lived another 350 years after the great flood. Noah's sons Shem, Ham, and Japheth and their wives came off the ark and set up housekeeping. Each of them had many children after they left the ark. That was exactly what God had told them to do. Those children were the beginning of the human population on Earth after the great flood. The animals that were on the ark had babies when they came back on dry land too. The earth was once again filled with life, just as God intended. The people lived and worked and worshiped God. They moved around and lived in various places. One group of people who lived near a place called Shinar made a poor choice, though.

The Tallest Building in the World
Genesis 11:1-9

After the great flood, all of the people who lived in the world spoke the same language. People who lived in various places could get together and everyone could understand what everyone else said. They could make plans or talk about the new world they lived in. They could talk about the great flood that their ancestors survived and the big ark Noah had built. They could talk about anything!

Apparently that was fine with God until one group of men had an idea. "Let's make bricks and bake them in ovens. That will make them strong enough that we can use them to build buildings." Before this new idea, buildings were made of stone. These men wanted to make buildings that were made of bricks that stacked on top of each other and were held together with mortar. Everyone thought this was a great idea so the men began making bricks and building the new city. They talked about their city as they worked. They planned what buildings they would make. As they were talking, someone had another idea. "Why don't we build a tower in our city that reaches all the way up into the heavens?" he said. "It will be the tallest building ever." All the other men thought this was a great idea. "We will be famous for our tall building," someone said. "We will

be so famous that no one will ever try to break us up or make us move to other cities. We will be powerful and will stay together here in our city because of our famous tower."

The men didn't ask God about their plan. Maybe they did not even care how He would feel about it. They should have known that God would not be happy about it. He did not like that the men were making plans of their own. God looked at the city and the very tall tower they were building. God was not happy with what He saw. "The problem is that these men all speak the same language, so nothing is impossible for them," God said. "They are building this tall tower now but next, they will be able to do anything they try." God knew He had to stop the men. He could not have them thinking they were more powerful than He is. God had a simple plan to stop the men. He made everyone begin speaking different languages. Men who one day could understand everything others said could not even talk to each other the next day. No one knew what anyone else was saying. Now they couldn't make plans. They couldn't even finish building their tall tower. Then God did just what the men had tried to prevent. He scattered them over all the earth. They all moved to different places. The place where the men had started building the tall tower was called Babel because God confused their language there. And the unfinished tower was called the Tower of Babel.

ABRAHAM'S STORY

About seven generations passed after the Tower of Babel. That was when God scattered people all over the world. He made the people speak different languages. Next, the story of God's people focused on the family of Terah. This was an important family. Terah had three sons: Abram, Nahor, and Haran. Haran was just a young man when he died. Haran had a son named Lot. The son named Abram married a beautiful woman named Sarai. They wanted to have a family. Unfortunately, Sarai could not have any children. One day Terah decided to move to the land of Canaan. He took his grandson, Lot with him. He also took Abram and Sarai with him. They walked and walked. They got to the village of Haran. The little family stayed in Haran a long time. In fact, they never moved on to Canaan. Terah died while the family lived in Haran.

Abram's Big Move *Genesis 12*

After Terah died, God had a special message for Abram. God told him to pack up his family and move away from Haran. God didn't tell Abram where he was moving to. He just told him to start traveling. God made a promise to Abram. He said, "I will make you the father of a great nation, Abram. I will bless you. You will be famous and you will be a real blessing to other people. All people on Earth will be blessed through you, Abram!"

Abram obeyed God and took his wife, Sarai, and his nephew, Lot, and left Haran. He also took his servants and all the animals he owned when they left Haran. They left Haran and walked through the land of Canaan. When they were close to a city called Shechem they stopped and set up camp. Many people lived in that area but God spoke to Abram again and said, "I am going to give this land to you and your children." Abram was very happy so he built an altar there to celebrate. Abram kept traveling because there

was a terrible famine in the land of Canaan. The famine made it very hard to find food. There was not a famine in Egypt though. That meant there was food there. So Abram kept going until his family reached Egypt. As they were crossing into that country, Abram suddenly thought of something. "Sarai," he said, "you are so beautiful that I'm worried about a problem we may have. I'm afraid that the Egyptians will see how beautiful you are and want you for their own. Since you are my wife, they will kill me so they can have you. So let's tell them that you are my sister instead of my wife. Then we can be sure they won't kill me."

So, Sarai told everyone that Abram was her brother instead of her husband. Sure enough, when the Egyptians saw how beautiful she was they ran to tell the Pharaoh. Of course, the Pharaoh wanted Sarai to become one of his wives. So Sarai went to live at his palace. Pharaoh gave Abram many wonderful, expensive presents in exchange for Sarai. He gave Abram sheep, cows, donkeys, and even servants.

But God knew what was going on. He knew that Sarai was Abram's wife and not his sister. He wasn't happy that Pharaoh had taken Abram's wife. God sent terrible plagues on Pharaoh's household. It wasn't long before Pharaoh figured out what had happened. "Why did you do this to me?" he asked Abram. "Why didn't you just tell me that Sarai was your wife? Take her and get out of here," Pharaoh said. In fact, Pharaoh sent an armed guard to lead them out of Egypt. Abram, Sarai, Lot, and all the servants were escorted out of the country.

Abram and Lot Go Separate Ways
Genesis 13

Abram rounded up his large herds of cattle. He gathered up his servants and all his possessions. Then Abram, Sarai, and Lot headed north out of Egypt. Lot was also very wealthy. He had large herds of cattle and sheep and many servants. They traveled to a place between Bethel and Ai. This was the place where Abram had previously built an altar to worship God. They stopped there and set up their tents. This area was very fertile with gardens and grasses for the animals to eat and rivers for them to drink from. But Abram and Lot's herds of cattle and flocks of sheep living together

meant there were very many animals in one place. There wasn't enough food and water to support both of their large herds. The men caring for the animals began to argue with each other. Abram's workers said, "Our master is more important. His animals should get the food and water." But Lot's workers thought that Abram's herds should go somewhere else so that Lot's animals could have the food and water. Their arguing got worse and worse until they were

arguing all the time. The herdsmen were all concerned about their animals having enough food and water.

Abram knew this arguing was not good so he went to talk with Lot. "This arguing has to stop," he said. "After all, we are related. We need to get along with each other. Here's my plan: You choose which piece of land you want to live on. Take whichever section you want. Then we will separate and I'll take my family and animals somewhere else. If you want

to move to some other place, I will stay here. But if you want to stay here, then I will move. It's up to you."

Lot looked at the beautiful Jordan Valley. It had lots of grasses and water. It was as beautiful and fertile as the land of Egypt. It was the best land around. So Lot chose that land for himself and his animals. He moved his family, servants, animals, and tents near a city called Sodom. The people of Sodom were very wicked. They sinned against God by the way they lived. Lot didn't care though. He knew it was the best land for his herds and flocks.

Abram stayed in the land of Canaan. God said to him, "Look around you. Look as far as your eye can see in every direction. I will give all of this land to you. It will belong to you and your children." God wasn't finished with His promises. He said, "I will give you children. You will have so many descendants that you won't even be able to count them. So go for a walk and see your new homeland." Abram did just that. Then he built an altar and worshiped God.

46

God's Promise to Abram *Genesis 14, 15*

A fter Lot left Abram and moved to the Jordan Valley, a war broke out there. Kings from five different areas banded together to fight against a king named Kedorlaomer and his allies. In the middle of the battle Lot was somehow captured. The kings took everything Lot owned. One man escaped and ran to tell Abram what had happened to Lot. Abram had to rescue his nephew. The king of Salem was happy that Abram defeated the evil kings. He offered to let Abram keep the wealth of all the people he had captured.

Abram refused though. He didn't want the king to be able to say that Abram's riches came from him. Abram wanted people to know that his wealth came from God!

When Abram returned home from rescuing Lot, God renewed His promise to Abram. "Do not ever be afraid, Abram. I will always protect you. You will have a wonderful reward for obeying me," God said.

But Abram was confused. "What good are all Your blessings to me: the wealth, the cattle, the sheep? I don't have a son to inherit any of my wealth. You are giving me all these riches, but it just means that my servant will inherit my things when I die."

"No," God said, "it will not be your servant who inherits your wealth. You will have a son of your own." God directed Abram to go outside and look up at the night sky. "Count the stars if you can," He said. "You will have as many descendants in your family as there are stars in the sky." There were too many stars for Abram to count! Abram believed God. He had faith in what God told him. Abram's faith made God happy.

But after he thought about it some, Abram wanted more proof. He asked God, "How can I really be sure that You will do what You say?" God told Abram to offer a special animal sacrifice. Abram did what God told him to do. He took some of the animals God requested, killed them, and divided their bodies down the middle. Afterwards he fell asleep and had a terrible nightmare. Vultures flew down to eat the animals but Abram chased them away. Then God said to him, "Your descendants will be in slavery for 400 years. Life will be very hard for them. But I will punish the nation that holds them as slaves. After four generations your descendants will be able to return to this land I'm giving you. I promise that you, Abram, will die at a ripe old age."

Later that night, Abram saw a pot filled with smoke and a fiery torch pass between the two parts of the animals. That meant that God was sealing the promise He had made to Abram. "Abram, I am giving you this land—all of it—and it will belong to your descendants forever. I promise!"

Angel Visitors *Genesis 18:1-15*

A bram and Sarai were now called Abraham and Sarah. God changed their names because Abraham would become the father of many nations. They continued traveling around, finding food and water for their animals. One place Abraham and Sarah set up their tent was near a small grove of oak trees. The trees gave them some shade from the hot desert sun. One day

50

about noontime Abraham was sitting near the opening to his tent when he noticed three men standing a little way off. He ran to them and said, "You may stop here and rest for a while, if you like. You can sit in the shade of these trees where it's a little cooler. My servants will get water to wash your feet. I'll get some food for you. Just stay and rest before you go on your way again."

The men agreed to stay for a while so Abraham ran inside the tent and told Sarah to bake some bread as quickly as she could. Then he ran out to his herds and chose a nice fat calf to have his servants cook. When the food was all ready Abraham served it to the men. While the men were eating they asked Abraham, "Where is your wife, Sarah?"

"She is inside the tent," Abraham answered.

Then one of the men said something that was totally amazing. "About this time next year," he said, "I will come back this way again. By that time, your wife, Sarah, will have a baby boy."

Sarah was standing near the opening of the tent and listening to the men talk. When she heard the man say that she was going to have a baby, she laughed to herself! She and Abraham were both very old—way too old to have a baby! "How can an old body like mine have a baby? It wore out a long time ago and Abraham is an old man too!"

God knew that Sarah was laughing at the news, so He asked Abraham, "Why did Sarah laugh? Why did she say that she is too old to have a baby? Does she think this is too hard for God? I'm telling you that a year from now, I will come back here and Sarah will have a baby." Sarah was scared to admit that she laughed at what God said so she denied that she had laughed. But God said, "That's not true, Sarah. You did laugh."

God Destroys Sodom   *Genesis 18:16–19:26*

When the three men left Abraham, they headed toward the city of Sodom. Abraham went with them part of the way. As they were walking God said to Abraham, "I have heard that the people of Sodom are very evil. I'm going to see for myself."

Abraham understood what God was planning to do so he courageously asked, "God, will You destroy all the people in Sodom—the innocent people along with the evil people? What if You find just 50 innocent people there? Will You still destroy the city or would You spare it for their sakes? If You destroy it, You would be treating the innocent people the same way You treat the guilty. You wouldn't do that, would You?"

The Lord replied, "If I find 50 innocent people then I will not destroy the city."

"Since I've started asking these questions, let me ask another one," Abraham said. "What if there are only 45 innocent people?"

"If I find 45 innocent people, I will save the city," God answered.

Abraham kept questioning God until he finally asked, "What if there are only 10?"

"I will save the city if I find 10 innocent people there," God said. Then the Lord left and Abraham returned to his tent.

That evening two angels came to Sodom and Lot met them at the entrance of the city. "Come to my house," Lot said to them. "You can stay for the night and then go on your way in the morning." But the angels said they would just spend the night in the city square. However, Lot insisted that they come home with him, so they did. He served them a wonderful dinner and then they got ready to rest for the night. Suddenly, all the men of Sodom showed up outside Lot's door. They had seen the strangers come to Lot's house and they shouted for Lot to send them out. Lot went out to try to reason with the men. But the men yelled, "Who do you think you are? You aren't one of us. We just let you live here. Send those men out right now!" They started to attack Lot but the angels yanked him back inside the house and bolted the door shut.

"You have to get out of this city," they said to Lot. "We are going to completely destroy it. The stink of the evil that goes on here has reached God and He won't put up with it any longer! Take your whole family and get out!"

When the sun was rising the next morning the angels grabbed Lot, his wife, and two daughters by the hands and rushed them out of Sodom. "Run to the mountains where you will be safe!" they cried.

"No, I don't want to go to the mountains," Lot said. "Let me go to that little town over there. Won't we be safe there?"

"Fine, go to that town and we won't destroy it. Now run and don't look back!" the angels said. Lot and his wife and daughters ran for the town just as fire began to rain down from the sky onto Sodom. The whole city burned to the ground. All the people, plants, and animals inside it burned up. Cities around Sodom that were also filled with evil people burned up too. Lot and his daughters were safe in the little town where the angels sent them. But Lot's wife disobeyed the angels. She looked back at Sodom as it burned and her body instantly turned into a pillar of salt.

Hagar and Ishmael Are Sent Away

Genesis 16:1-4, 15; 21:1-21

God had promised a long time ago to give Abraham and Sarah children, but they were both very old and still did not have any. So Sarah decided to take matters into her own hands. She sent her maid to Abraham and said, "Have a baby with Hagar. Maybe she will have a son and we can raise him as our son." The maid did have a baby boy and

named him Ishmael. But this boy was not part of God's plan for Abraham's descendants.

A little later Sarah had a son just as God promised. Her son was named Isaac, which means laughter. Remember, Sarah had laughed when God said that she would have a baby. Once Isaac was born, Sarah became jealous of Hagar and her son, Ishmael.

When Isaac was still quite young Abraham threw a party for him. At the party Sarah heard Ishmael making fun of Isaac. That made her angry. "I insist that you send Hagar and her son away from here!" she told Abraham. "I don't want that boy to share in my son's inheritance!" Abraham was very upset by Sarah's demands. After all, Ishmael was his son too. He hadn't really done anything wrong.

But God told Abraham it was OK to send Hagar and Ishmael away. "Isaac is the son through whom I will keep my covenant with you," God said. "But I promise to watch over Hagar and Ishmael. I will even build a nation from Ishmael's descendants because he is your son too."

Abraham got up early the next morning and gathered some food and water for Hagar to take as she and Ishmael left. Then he sadly sent Hagar and her son away from his camp. Hagar and Ishmael wandered aimlessly for a long time. They really had nowhere to go. When their water ran out, Hagar left Ishmael sitting in the shade of a bush. She walked a short distance away from him and sat down too. "I can't stand to watch my son die," she cried. Tears ran down her face.

Meanwhile, Ishmael was crying and God heard him. God's angel called down to Hagar, "Don't be afraid, Hagar. God has heard your son's cries. Go comfort your little boy. God promises to make him into a great nation!" Then God miraculously showed Hagar a well that was filled with water. She filled the jar Abraham had given her with water and gave Ishmael a drink. Ishmael grew up to be a strong young man. Hagar arranged a marriage for him with a young Egyptian woman.

THE STORY OF ISAAC

When God makes a promise, He keeps it! God promised Abraham and Sarah that He would give them a huge family. But the older they got, the more they wondered if they had misunderstood Him. Abraham and Sarah tried to make God's promise come true by doing some things themselves, but they found out that it was not a good idea to take matters into their own hands. Eventually Sarah did have a baby. Her child was a boy named Isaac. God had kept His promise. He always does. But life didn't settle into an easy pattern for Abraham, Sarah, and Isaac. God had some important lessons to teach each of them.

Abraham's Difficult Test *Genesis 22*

Abraham and Sarah waited a long, long time for God to keep His promise to give them lots of descendants. He had promised them as many descendants as there were stars in the sky! Finally, when Abraham was 100 years old, Sarah had a baby boy. They named him Isaac. He was the proof to them that God keeps His promises. A few years after Isaac was born, God asked Abraham to do something very, very difficult.

"Abraham, take your son, Isaac—the boy you love so very much—and go up to the mountains. I want you to sacrifice Isaac as an offering to me." Abraham didn't argue with God. He obeyed Him. Abraham tried to always obey God.

The next morning Abraham got up early and saddled his donkey. He took two servants and his son, Isaac, with him. He chopped enough wood to build a fire for a burnt offering. He brought a pot of fire to burn the offering. He led the little group to the place where God directed him to go. On the third day of traveling Abraham told the two servants to stay with the donkey while he and Isaac went on a little farther. "We will worship God, then come right back," he told them.

Abraham piled the wood for the fire on Isaac's strong, young shoulders. He carried the knife and the pot of fire himself. As they walked along Isaac noticed something. "Father?" he said.

"Yes, my son," Abraham answered.

"We have the wood and the fire for the offering but where is the lamb to sacrifice?" Isaac asked.

"God will provide the lamb," Abraham answered.

When they got to the place God directed them to, Abraham stopped and built an altar and put the wood on it. Then he tied up his son, Isaac, and laid him on the altar. Abraham took the knife and slowly lifted it up to kill

his son as a sacrifice to God. But just at that moment an angel shouted to him from Heaven, "Abraham! Abraham!"

"Yes," Abraham answered, "I'm listening."

"Put the knife down," the angel said. "Do not hurt the boy in any way for now I know that you fear God completely. You didn't even hold back your beloved son from Him."

Right at that moment Abraham saw a ram caught by its horns in a nearby bush. So he took the ram and sacrificed it as the offering to God in place of his son. Abraham named that place on the mountain "The Lord Will Provide."

Then the angel called to Abraham again. "God says that because you have obeyed Him so completely He will multiply your descendants to be as many as the stars in the sky and the grains of sand on the seashore. Through your descendants all the nations of the earth will be blessed. All of this will happen because you have obeyed me."

Abraham and Isaac went back to where the servants were waiting and they all returned home. Abraham lived a long time after that.

A Bride for Isaac *Genesis 24*

G od blessed Abraham throughout his life. When Abraham was a very old man he called one of his oldest, most trusted servants to his side. "Promise me in God's name that you will not let my son, Isaac, marry one of the local girls. I do not want him to marry a Canaanite girl. Instead, I want you to go to my homeland and find a wife for Isaac."

"What if I can't find a young woman who is willing to leave her home and

family to travel here and marry your son?" the servant asked. "Is it alright if I take Isaac back to your homeland to marry and live there among your relatives?"

"No!" Abraham shouted. "He must never leave this land. God himself brought me to this land and promised to give it to me and to my children. God will send His angel ahead of you. He will help you find a wife for Isaac from among my people. She will be willing to come here to Canaan and marry my son. However, if you find a suitable woman but she is not willing to come here, then you are free from this task. Under no circumstances are you to take Isaac there!"

The servant promised that he would follow Abraham's instructions. He loaded 10 camels with gifts and left for Abraham's homeland. When he got to the village where Abraham's brother lived, he made the camels kneel down beside a well outside the village. It was just at the time of the evening when the women came out to draw water from the well. "O God," the servant prayed, "help me find a wife for my master's son. This is my request: I will ask one of the women for a drink. If she says, 'Yes and I will also water your camels,' then I will know that she is the one You have chosen to be Isaac's wife."

While he was still praying, a pretty young woman named Rebekah came to the well. She was the daughter of Abraham's nephew. As Rebekah filled her water jug the servant ran over to her.

"Please give me a drink," he said.

"Certainly," Rebekah answered, "and I will also get some water for your camels to drink." After the servant had a drink, she emptied the rest of the water into the camel's water trough. Then she went to get more water for them. She kept bringing water to the camels until they had all they wanted. When the camels were finished, the servant gave Rebekah a gold ring and two gold bracelets.

"Who is your father?" the servant asked. "Would we be able to stay with him for the night?"

"My father is Bethuel," Rebekah answered. "I'm sure you could stay for the night. We have plenty of room and we have straw and food for your camels."

The servant fell to the ground and praised God because he knew Rebekah was the woman God had chosen to be Isaac's wife. He went home with her and asked her family's permission to take her to Canaan to marry Isaac. They agreed to let her go if she wanted to. Rebekah was happy to go with the servant so he took her to meet Isaac. Rebekah and Isaac were married and Isaac loved her very much.

JACOB'S STORY

Isaac and Rebekah got married and God poured out His blessings on Isaac, the son God had promised to give Abraham. The story of God's work continued with the life of Isaac and his children. Two of Isaac's children were twin boys. Esau and Jacob became the focus of God's story. They both had problems as young men. Both of them made some bad choices. Jacob lied and did bad things. But when he grew up, Jacob became the father of 12 sons who led the 12 tribes of Israel.

Esau's Bad Choice *Genesis 25:21-34*

Isaac and Rebekah were very happy together except for the fact that they did not have any children. Isaac asked God to please give them a child. God answered Isaac's prayer and Rebekah became pregnant with twins! The two children seemed to fight when they were still inside her. She asked the Lord about it and He told her that they were two boys who would grow up to lead nations that would fight each other. He also told her that the older boy's family would end up serving the family of the younger boy. That was just the opposite of what should happen in their culture. Usually the oldest boy had all the power in the family. That came with the birthright which gave the oldest boy leadership of the family when the father died. It also gave the oldest boy a greater inheritance of the father's wealth. Finally the twins

were born. The first boy had lots of red hair. He was named Esau which means "hair." The second boy was born holding on to the heel of his brother. Isaac and Rebekah named him Jacob which means "one who grasps the heel."

The boys were very different as far as what they liked to do. Esau loved to be outside and Jacob liked to stay inside. When they grew up Esau became a very good hunter. He loved being out in the wilderness and hunting food for the family to eat. Jacob liked to stay at home and cook. Isaac especially liked Esau because he brought home food he had hunted for the family to eat. Rebekah liked Jacob more.

One day Jacob was at home making some stew while Esau was out hunting. When Esau got home he was tired and very hungry. "Give me some of that stew

you're cooking," he said to his brother.

"Sure," said Jacob, "but you have to give me your birthright in exchange for the stew." Jacob was trying to trick his brother into giving away his birthright which was very important. Jacob wanted to be in charge of the family when Isaac died. He didn't want to have to serve Esau for the rest of his life.

"I'm starving!" Esau cried. "You can have the birthright. It won't do me any good anyway if I die from hunger."

Jacob held the bowl of stew away from Esau and said, "Promise me the birthright is mine and I will give you this bowl of steaming hot stew."

"I promise. I promise!" Esau shouted. He grabbed the bowl of stew from Jacob and pushed his brother aside. Esau gobbled the food down and then went about his business as usual. He didn't even care that he had just given up his birthright. Jacob knew that something important had just happened.

Jacob's Mean Trick *Genesis 27:1-41*

Isaac called his oldest son, Esau, to him. "I'm an old man and I don't know how much longer I will live. So take your bow and arrow and go hunt for wild game. When you have some, bring it back and cook it just the way I like. Bring the food to me and I will eat it, then I will give you the blessing of the firstborn son of a family."

Esau grabbed his bow and arrow and left. But Rebekah had overheard their conversation. She didn't want Esau to get Isaac's blessing. She wanted Jacob to have it. So she came up with a plan. "Jacob!" she called. "I heard your father tell Esau to make his favorite meal. After your father eats it he will bless Esau. I want you to have that blessing, so do exactly what I tell you to do. Bring me two young goats and I'll cook them the way your father likes. Then you take the food to him. He will eat it and then bless you instead of Esau!"

But Jacob didn't think his mother's plan would work. "Mother, even though Father's eyesight is very bad, he will know that I'm not Esau. What if he touches me? My skin is smooth and Esau's skin is hairy. Father won't be fooled. Then he will curse me instead of blessing me."

"Just do what I tell you to do," Rebekah insisted. So Jacob followed his mother's instructions. He brought the goats to her and she cooked them. Then she told Jacob to put on Esau's best clothes. She strapped pieces of hairy goat skin on Jacob's arms and hands and around his neck. That would make his skin feel more like his brother's skin if Isaac should touch him. Jacob took the food to his father and said, "Father?"

"Yes," Isaac answered. "Who is there? Esau or Jacob?"

"It's Esau, your oldest boy," Jacob lied. "I've brought your favorite dish for you to enjoy. So sit up and enjoy your dinner then you can give me your blessing."

"Come over here," Isaac said. "I want to touch you and make sure that you are really Esau." Jacob went to his father and Isaac touched his arms and his neck. The old man thought, *The voice I hear is Jacob's, but the hands feel like Esau's hands.*

"Are you really Esau?" he asked once again.

"Yes, Father, of course I am," Jacob lied.

"Then bring me the meat," Isaac said. Jacob gave him the food and he ate it. Then he said, "Give me a kiss, my son."

When Jacob kissed his father, Isaac smelled the scent of the clothing and was finally convinced that it was Esau standing before him. "May God always bless your crops and give you good harvests," he said. "May many nations become your servants. May you be the master of your brothers. May all your mother's sons bow before you. All who curse you are cursed and all who bless you are blessed." The blessing was now given . . . to Jacob, not Esau.

When Esau returned with the food he had hunted, he prepared it and took it to his father. "I'm here with your food, Father," he said. "Eat it and then give me your blessing."

"Who are you?" Isaac asked.

"Your son, Esau," Esau answered.

Isaac began to shake because he knew what had happened. "I've already given the blessing," he whispered, "I gave it to your brother."

Esau began to cry, "Father, bless me too! Please give me a blessing!"

"I can't," Isaac said, "I've blessed Jacob and now you must serve him. But I will tell you that even though you must serve him for a while, you will one day shake free from him."

Esau was filled with hatred toward his brother and he promised himself that he would kill Jacob one day.

Jacob's Strange Dream *Genesis 28:10-22*

Esau threatened to kill his brother, Jacob, for stealing the blessing of the firstborn son from their father, Isaac, so Jacob ran for his life. Actually, his mother said that it might be a good idea for him to go away for a while until his brother calmed down. So she asked Isaac to send Jacob to visit his uncle in Paddan-aram and find a wife there from their own people. Jacob

left immediately on the long journey to his uncle's house. When night came he looked around for a good place to sleep. When he found a place, he set up camp and found a smooth stone to use for a pillow. Tired from his long journey, he fell right to sleep. As he was sleeping, Jacob started to dream about a giant stairway that reached from Earth all the way to Heaven. There were angels of God

going up and down the stairway.

God himself stood at the top of the staircase and He said, "I am the Lord, the God of your grandfather, Abraham, and the God of your father, Isaac. The ground you are sleeping on will be yours, Jacob. I give it to you and all your descendants. You will have as many descendants as there is dust on the earth! Yes, they will cover the land from east to west and north to south. All the nations of the earth will be blessed through your descendants, Jacob. Also, I promise to take care of you and protect you. I will be with you wherever you go and someday I will bring you back to this land. I will always be with you!"

Then Jacob woke up and he remembered the whole dream. "God is in this very place," he thought. "I didn't even know that I set up camp in the house of God! What an amazing place this is!" The next morning when he woke up, Jacob took the smooth stone that he had used as a pillow and set it upright on the ground as a memorial. He poured oil over it and named the place "Bethel" which means "house of God."

Jacob was amazed at the promises God had given him. He made a promise too. He said, "If God will be with me and protect me and give me food and clothing, and if He will someday get me safely back to my father's house, then He will certainly be my God! This memorial that I've made from the stone will become a place to worship God and I promise to give back to God a tenth of everything He gives me!"

Jacob Wrestles with God *Genesis 32:22-32*

Jacob found a wife from his uncle's family. Actually he found two: Rachel and Leah. They were both the daughters of Laban. Jacob and his wives stayed with Laban,

and Jacob worked for his father-in-law. His wives had babies and Jacob's family grew quite large. But after a while, Laban's sons began complaining about Jacob because they thought he was getting

too much from their father. They even accused Jacob of stealing from their father. That's about the time that Jacob noticed that Laban didn't seem to like him much anymore. God noticed Laban's attitude too. He told Jacob to take his wives and his children and go back to the land of his father, Isaac. Jacob was happy to do that and his wives were glad to leave their family too. Jacob loaded up everything he owned and headed for home. Along the way some angels of God came to meet Jacob. They told him that his brother, Esau, was traveling toward him. Jacob was frightened because years before Esau had pledged to kill him. He was sure Esau was still angry enough to want to kill him. Jacob set up camp and worked to prepare a very generous gift to send to Esau.

During the night Jacob had the gift all ready for Esau and he decided to send his two wives and 11 sons on across the river. He stayed behind all alone. A man showed up and began wrestling with Jacob. They fought and struggled until the morning dawned. When the man saw that daylight was coming he realized that he couldn't defeat Jacob so

he touched Jacob and knocked his hip right out of the socket. He said, "It's dawn. Let me go."

"No," Jacob said, "I won't let you go until you bless me."

"What's your name?" the man asked.

"My name is Jacob," he answered through his pain.

"You will not be called Jacob anymore. From now on you will be called Israel because you have wrestled with both man and God and have won," the man said.

"What is your name?" Jacob asked the man. The man didn't answer him but he did bless Jacob. That's when Jacob knew that he had been wrestling with God! He named that place "Peniel" which means "face of God." Jacob knew that he had seen God face to face—yet he hadn't died. That was amazing.

The sun came up as Jacob left Peniel to meet his brother. He was limping because of his hip. For that reason, to this day, the people of Israel do not eat meat from near the hip socket.

Jacob Meets Esau *Genesis 32:1-18; 33*

Shortly after Jacob and his wives and children left Laban's home, they heard that Esau was traveling toward them. Esau and Jacob had not seen each other for several years but Jacob remembered that Esau had threatened to kill him the last time they had been together. Jacob heard that Esau had an army of 400 men traveling with him. Jacob was so frightened that he divided his family into two groups so that if Esau attacked one group the other one could escape. "God," Jacob prayed, "remember that You promised to take care of me. You're the one who told me to go back to my homeland. Please protect me from Esau. I'm afraid that he is planning to kill me and my wives and children. Remember, God, that You promised that I would have many, many descendants, so please, God, protect us!"

Jacob set up camp right where he was and began pulling together a gift for Esau of goats, ewes, rams, camels, cows, bulls, and donkeys. He had his servants take the gift on ahead to give

to Esau and tell him that his brother, Jacob, was coming. He hoped that the generous gift he sent would calm Esau's anger toward him.

The morning after Jacob wrestled with God, he got up and started on the journey again. Far off in the distance he saw Esau coming toward him with his army of 400 men. Jacob quickly put his family in a long column. He put his favorite wife, Rachel, and her children last. His favorite son, Joseph, was the very last person in the line. Jacob went out to meet his brother. As he got close to Esau, Jacob dropped to the ground and bowed before his brother. He did this seven times. To Jacob's surprise, Esau ran to him and grabbed him in a big hug. He kissed Jacob and cried with joy. Jacob also cried with joy at seeing his brother again.

"Who are all these people?" Esau asked as he saw the long line of people.

"These people are my family—my wives and my children. God has been very generous to me," Jacob said.

"Why did you send all the goats and cattle to me?" Esau asked.

"They were gifts for you. I hoped that they would make you less angry with me," Jacob answered.

"I have plenty of wealth of my own, so keep your gifts," Esau told him.

"I really want you to have them," Jacob said. "It is a true joy to see your friendly smile so please keep the gifts. God has been very generous to me. He has blessed me with great wealth," Jacob insisted. Esau finally agreed to keep the gifts.

"Let's keep going," Esau said. "Follow me and I will lead the way."

"No," Jacob said, "I have very young children who couldn't keep up. I'll travel at my own pace with my family and meet you at Seir." Esau left but Jacob went as far as Succoth and built a house for his family.

THE LIFE OF JOSEPH

Jacob had 12 sons. Of course, he loved all his boys but his favorite son was Joseph, the next to the youngest son. The 10 older boys knew that Joseph was their father's favorite and it made them very jealous. Jacob's favoritism caused Joseph a lot of problems with his brothers. Jacob didn't intend for that to happen but it did. God meant for all the problems to end up bringing good things to Joseph's life. God had an important plan for Joseph.

A Coat of Many Colors *Genesis 37:1-5*

Jacob and his wives and children returned to the land of Canaan where Jacob's father, Isaac, had lived. Jacob was glad to be home and glad to be away from Laban, the father of his two wives. Laban had cheated him and threatened his life.

Jacob had 12 sons who were very important in God's story. Each of those sons grew up to lead one of the 12 tribes of Israel. Jacob loved all of his sons, but his favorite was Joseph, the next to the youngest son. Part of the reason that Jacob loved Joseph so much was that Joseph was born when Jacob was an old man and he loved Joseph's mother, Rachel, best.

As in any Hebrew family, each of Jacob's sons had jobs to do. Joseph's job, along with a couple of his brothers, was to watch his father's sheep. But Joseph knew that he was his father's favorite son so he added one little chore to watching the sheep. He also watched his brothers! If his brothers did bad things or misbehaved, Joseph reported it to his father. That made him very unpopular with his brothers. They didn't trust Joseph and they didn't like him at all.

Jacob either didn't notice how his other sons felt or he just didn't care. It seemed like whatever Joseph did just made Jacob love him more. He gave Joseph many gifts that he didn't give his other sons. One day he gave Joseph a very special, beautiful gift. It was a new coat, but not just any coat. This one had many bright and beautiful colors on it. When Joseph wore it, people could see him coming from far away. Each time his brothers saw Joseph wearing that coat they were reminded once again of

how their father loved him more than any of them. They hated Joseph more and more, especially the oldest brothers who should have been the honored sons in the family. None of them could find a single good thing to say about Joseph. When they were together they talked about how much they hated him.

Joseph's Unusual Dreams *Genesis 37:6-17*

Joseph often got his brothers into trouble because he reported to their dad when they were misbehaving or goofing off. But he wasn't really trying to get them into trouble. He did not seem to know how much they hated him. If he *did* know then he probably would not have done this next thing.

One night Joseph had a dream that was really amazing. Perhaps he should have kept the dream to himself, but he

didn't. He ran and told his brothers the whole thing. "Brothers! Listen to this dream I had. We were all out in a field tying bundles of grain together. All of a sudden, my bundle stood up tall and all of your bundles circled around it and bowed down to it! It was amazing!"

Joseph's brothers were not very happy to hear about this dream. "So, what are you saying? Do you think you're going to be our king?" They made fun of him and laughed at his ridiculous dream. But his dream made them hate him more.

The next night Joseph had another dream which he also reported to his brothers. "This time the sun, moon, and stars bowed down to me!" He told his father about this dream. As much as his father loved Joseph, he didn't appreciate the dream either.

"Are you saying that your mother and I are going to bow down to you?" Jacob asked. Joseph's brothers hated him even more because of this second dream, but Jacob didn't hate him.

Instead, he wondered if the dream had real meaning and what it might be.

Not long after Joseph's two dreams, Jacob sent his other sons to take his flocks to a field near the town of Shechem. They were gone for quite a while and Jacob had heard no reports from them. So he sent Joseph to check on them and report back to him. When Joseph got to Shechem he wasn't exactly sure where to find his brothers and he wandered around from field to field looking for them. A man noticed Joseph and thought that he might be lost so he asked Joseph what he was looking for.

"I'm trying to find my brothers and their flocks," Joseph answered. "Have you seen them anywhere?"

"Yes," the man answered. "I saw them, but they are no longer here. I heard them say they were going to take the flocks to Dothan." Joseph thanked the man and headed for Dothan to find his brothers. Joseph's life took an unusual turn when he got there.

Joseph Becomes a Slave *Genesis 37:18-36*

Joseph traveled to Dothan to find his brothers so that he could report back to his father how they were doing. Jacob asked him to do that, but Joseph's brothers were not happy to see him. When he was still a long way off his brothers saw Joseph walking toward them. It was hard to miss his brightly colored coat—a special gift to him from their father. Just seeing that coat again made them angry. So the brothers huddled together and came up with an evil plan. They decided to kill their brother, Joseph, because

their father loved him best and because of his dreams about them bowing down to him. "We can kill him and throw his body into a deep pit then tell Father that a wild animal ate him." That was their plan. But one brother, Reuben, came to Joseph's rescue. He didn't want his younger brother to be killed.

"Wait, brothers. I don't like this plan. Why should we have his blood on

our souls? Let's just throw him into the pit and let him die on his own. The pit is deep enough that he can't climb out so eventually he will die without us touching him." Reuben's secret plan was to go back after the brothers had left, rescue Joseph from the pit, and return him to their father. The brothers agreed to Reuben's plan.

When Joseph finally reached them, the brothers grabbed him, pulled off his coat of many colors, and threw him into the deep pit. Joseph cried out for them to help him but they ignored him and sat down to eat. Then one of the brothers noticed a long line of camels off in the distance. It was a group of traders heading to Egypt to sell their spices and perfumes. "Hmmm," Judah said, "listen, we don't really have anything to gain from Joseph dying. We just want him out of our lives, right? What if we sell him to those traders and they take him to Egypt and sell him into slavery? We can still tell Father that a wild animal got him but he will be out of our lives. What do you think?" All the brothers talked about this idea and decided it was a good one because they would be rid of Joseph but they wouldn't have his death on their conscience.

When the traders were nearby the brothers called them over. They sold their brother for 20 pieces of silver and the traders tied him up and took him to Egypt. Reuben, the brother who wanted to free Joseph, was gone when all of this happened. So when he came back to rescue Joseph, he was surprised to find the pit empty. Reuben was very upset and went to find his brothers. With tears rolling down his cheeks he said, "Joseph is gone! What do I do now?"

The brothers already had a plan though. They killed a goat and dipped Joseph's brightly colored coat in the blood. Then they went home and showed the bloody coat to their father. "We found this coat in a field," they lied. "Can you identify it as Joseph's?"

Jacob recognized the coat at once and he was heartbroken. "Yes, it is my son's coat. A wild animal must have eaten him. Joseph must be dead." Jacob was heartbroken and mourned for his favorite son for a long time. The whole family tried to comfort him but he would not listen to any of them. "I will die grieving for my son," he said.

Meanwhile, the group of traders arrived in Egypt and sold Joseph as a slave.

Joseph in Potiphar's House *Genesis 39:1-6*

J oseph must have been very confused as the traders took him from his brothers and began the long trip to Egypt. Why had this happened to him? Why did his brothers do this to him? Did he have any idea how jealous his brothers were of him?

When the traders arrived in Egypt they immediately put Joseph up for sale as a slave. He went from being the favorite son of Jacob to being a lowly slave. But things were going to get worse for him. Joseph was a strong, good-looking young boy so he probably brought a

good price. A man named Potiphar bought Joseph to be one of his many slaves. Potiphar was the captain of the guard in the king's palace so he was an important, powerful, and rich man.

Joseph was put to work in Potiphar's house doing jobs that he may never have done before. But Joseph didn't complain. He didn't fight what had happened to him, though he must have wondered why his own brothers would do something as terrible as selling him into slavery. Joseph worked hard! He did every job assigned to him as well as he could do it. He was honest and respectful. He did this because God was with him. Joseph gained strength and confidence from knowing that he wasn't alone—God knew what was happening. God blessed Joseph in all he did and Potiphar noticed how hard his new slave worked. He noticed that Joseph didn't steal things from his house. He saw that Joseph was truthful and showed respect. Joseph quickly became a favorite of Potiphar and was rewarded with a promotion. Potiphar put Joseph in charge of all the slaves who worked in Potiphar's house. Joseph was in charge of the household and all of Potiphar's business deals. He managed everything that happened in the house. He managed the field workers and the workers who took care of the animals. He had a lot of responsibility. This high position showed that Potiphar trusted Joseph with his home, his possessions, and his family. With Joseph in charge, everything in Potiphar's house ran smoothly. His crops and animals did well. Potiphar didn't have to worry about anything. Joseph took care of it all. Things were turning out pretty well for Joseph, but his situation was about to take a turn for the worse.

Joseph Goes to Prison *Genesis 39:19–40:1-23*

Joseph worked hard as the head slave in Potiphar's house. His master was very pleased with everything Joseph did. But a problem developed for the young slave.

Potiphar's wife began flirting with Joseph. She thought he was very handsome and she wanted Joseph to do things that he knew were wrong. When Joseph refused to do what she wanted, Potiphar's

wife told horrible lies about Joseph to her husband. She accused him of doing the very things he had refused to do! Potiphar was very angry with Joseph so he had him thrown in prison. One minute Joseph was running Potiphar's whole household and the next minute he was in jail. But God was still with Joseph and He helped Joseph be a model prisoner. Joseph worked hard and was always respectful. The jailers noticed Joseph. Before very long, the chief jailer put Joseph in charge of all the other prisoners. The chief jailer's job was much easier because Joseph took care of everything.

A little while later the Egyptian Pharaoh got very upset with his chief cupbearer and his chief baker. He had them thrown in jail and they ended up in the same jail as Joseph. One night each of them had very disturbing dreams that they didn't understand. The next day Joseph saw that each of these men seemed to be upset by something. He asked them what was wrong and they each told him they had bad dreams. Joseph asked to hear their dreams and when they told him, God helped him explain the meaning of the dreams. He told the cupbearer that he would be freed from jail and would return to his job as cupbearer to the Pharaoh. Joseph told the baker that he also would be freed from jail but after he was set free the Pharaoh would have him killed. The cupbearer and baker were thankful to know what their dreams meant, but the baker certainly hoped that Joseph was wrong. A short time later both of those men were released from jail, just as Joseph had said they would be. When they were released, the cupbearer was restored to his job for the Pharaoh. But the Pharaoh ordered that the baker be killed, just as Joseph had said. Joseph asked the cupbearer to please remember how he had helped him by interpreting the dream and to help him get released from jail too. But once he was free, the cupbearer forgot all about Joseph.

Joseph Is in Charge! *Genesis 41*

Two years after the cupbearer was released, the Pharaoh of Egypt had a dream that he couldn't understand. It woke him up and he was upset about what it might mean. The Pharaoh fell back asleep and had a second dream that upset him even more. The two dreams bothered him so much that he called in all his wise men, advisers, and magicians and commanded them to interpret the dreams for him. None of them could tell him what the dreams meant.

Just then the cupbearer remembered

Joseph. "Pharaoh, when I was in your jail I had a dream that I couldn't understand. There was another prisoner there who told me the exact meaning of my dream. Everything he said came true; for me and also for your chief baker."

Pharaoh sent for Joseph at once. After cleaning up and changing clothes, Joseph came to see the Pharaoh. "I have been told that you can explain dreams," the Pharaoh said to Joseph.

"No," Joseph answered, "that is not completely true. I can't explain your dream, but God can."

That was good enough for Pharaoh, so he told Joseph all about his two dreams. "Both dreams mean the same thing," Joseph said. "They mean that Egypt will have seven good years of many crops and immediately seven years of famine will follow. I think you should choose the wisest man in Egypt and put him in charge of saving and planning for the seven bad years. That way you will have enough food to get your nation through the seven bad years."

Pharaoh thought Joseph's idea was a good one. He met with his advisers to choose a wise man to lead the plan. As they talked, Pharaoh had an idea, "Who would be better than the very man who came up with this plan?" he asked. Pharaoh wanted Joseph in the position! "Joseph, you will manage my household and organize all my people. Only I myself will have more authority than you in all of Egypt." He gave Joseph new clothes and put his own ring on Joseph's finger. Joseph went from being a prisoner to being the second in command in all of Egypt.

So God's plan for Joseph was put into action. For the seven good years Joseph saved and stored food and grain. After seven years the storehouses were filled to overflowing. So when the seven bad years of famine came and people in neighboring nations were starving, Egypt had plenty of food. People from other countries came to Egypt to try to buy food. Every person who came had to speak to Joseph.

Joseph's Family Reunion *Genesis 42; 45:1-15*

Famine struck Egypt and all the lands around it. For seven years no crops would grow and people could not find food anywhere. The news that Egypt had food in its storehouses spread quickly. People came from many nations to ask Joseph if they could buy food. One group of people who came was Joseph's 10 older brothers. His younger brother, Benjamin, stayed home with their father. When the brothers came before Joseph, he recognized them immediately. But they didn't know who Joseph was. They thought their brother was a slave, not a ruler. Joseph pretended not to know who they were. He asked, "Who are you and where have you come from?"

"We are the sons of Jacob and we have come from the land of Canaan to buy grain," the brothers answered.

"No, I know better. I know you are here to spy on my land," Joseph said. Joseph insisted that they were lying. He said he would only believe their story if they went back and got their youngest brother. So he put all the brothers in jail for three days. Then Joseph allowed all of the brothers but one to return to Canaan and get Benjamin. The brothers agreed to do so. As they talked with each other, they thought that this was all happening to them because of what they had done to their brother, Joseph. The brothers didn't know that Joseph, who was listening to them talk, could understand everything they said. He learned that his brothers felt bad about what they did to him. Simeon was the brother chosen to stay behind while the others hurried back to get Benjamin.

Joseph gave them grain to take back to their families. They paid him for the grain, but Joseph had the money put into their bags of grain. They didn't find the money until they got back to Canaan. They were very frightened that Joseph would think they had stolen the grain so they waited until the grain was gone to return to Egypt.

When the brothers returned with Benjamin, Joseph had another plan. He invited all the brothers to eat with him. The brothers were afraid to go into Joseph's house. As soon as they got inside they confessed to the manager about the money. "Don't worry," he told them, "your God must have taken care of you. We got our money. That's all that matters." When Joseph came in, he asked the brothers about their father. They assured him that their father was in good health. Then he asked to meet their youngest brother. Joseph was overcome with emotion when he saw Benjamin. He had to leave the room. When he returned, Joseph told the brothers where to sit at the table. They were very surprised when he sat them in the right order—oldest to youngest!

Eventually, Joseph could not keep his secret any longer. "Brothers, I am Joseph. I am the one you sold into slavery!" The brothers were terrified. They thought Joseph would throw them all into an Egyptian prison. But he promised them that he would not. "You meant evil for me but God turned it into good. He put me into this position so that I could be here to save your lives. Go back to Canaan and get our father. Bring your families here to Egypt so that I can take care of all of you." Joseph kissed each of his brothers, including young Benjamin whom he was thrilled to see.

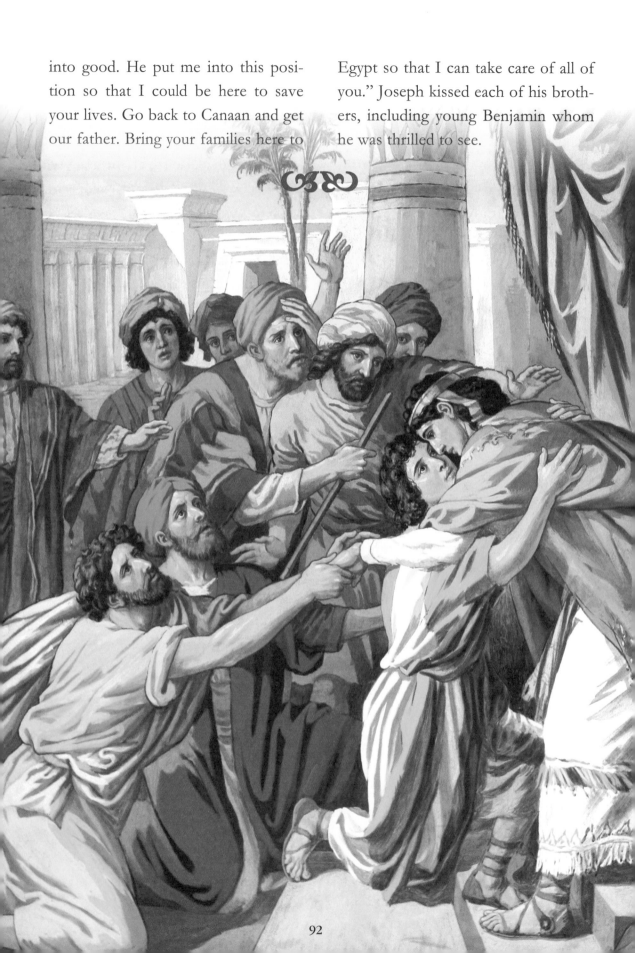

THE STORY OF MOSES

Joseph's success in Egypt made him very popular with the Pharaoh. Because of him the Hebrew people were protected from problems. But then Joseph died and a new Pharaoh came into power. This Pharaoh didn't know anything about Joseph. He didn't know what Joseph had done for Egypt. He was very nervous about all the Hebrews living in his country. He was worried that they might work together and try to take over Egypt. So the Egyptians made the Hebrews their slaves. They were mean slave masters and forced the Hebrew people to make bricks by hand. They made them work long hours in the fields. But God hadn't forgotten His people. He had an amazing plan to rescue them.

Moses Is Born and Rescued! *Exodus 2:1-10*

K ill every Hebrew baby boy that is born," the Egyptian Pharaoh ordered. The midwives could let the girl babies live. The Pharaoh didn't want any more Hebrew men in Egypt, so he solved the problem by not allowing more boys to live. But the midwives feared God so they didn't obey the Pharaoh. That made him angry so he ordered his people to grab all the Hebrew boy babies and throw them into the Nile River.

One Hebrew couple from the tribe of Levi had a baby boy during this time. He was a beautiful baby and his mother could not stand the idea of him being killed. She believed God had great work

for him to do. The couple hid the baby in their home for three months and managed to keep him quiet enough that no one knew about him. By then his cries were loud enough that his mother knew he would be discovered. But the brave mother had an idea. She wove a little basket from the tall grasses that grew along the edge of the Nile River. Then she covered the basket with tar so it would be waterproof. She put her precious baby boy in the basket and placed it in the river.

"Stay here and watch what happens to your baby brother," the mother told her daughter, Miriam. The young girl hid nearby and watched the little basket floating in the water.

A little while later the Egyptian princess came down to bathe in the river. She had many servants with her. The princess saw the little basket bobbing in the water and sent one of her servant girls to get it. When she opened the basket the small baby was crying and that touched her heart. "This is a Hebrew baby," she said. The princess decided right then to keep the baby as her own.

Miriam watched this all happening. Then she had an idea. She ran up to the princess and asked, "Would you like me to find a Hebrew woman to care for this baby for you?" The princess thought that was a great idea so Miriam raced back to her own home!

"Mother, come quickly!" Miriam shouted. "The princess has found our baby. She is going to keep him but she wants a Hebrew woman to care for him while he is so young. Come, Mother! You can take care of our baby and he will be safe!"

So the baby's own mother cared for him and the princess never knew that the baby belonged to the nursemaid. She even paid the mother for her work. When the child was old enough he went to live in the palace with the princess. She named him *Moses* because that means "drawn out of the water."

God Speaks from a Burning Bush

Exodus 3:1–4:17

Moses' mother was right when she thought God had a special job for her little boy. God saved Moses from Pharaoh for a reason. Moses grew up to become a shepherd. One day he was taking care of his father-in-law's flock of sheep and he took the flock into the wilderness near Mt. Sinai. Moses was watching the sheep eat the grass when suddenly the angel of the Lord called to him. Moses looked around and saw a bush that seemed to be on fire. He was amazed because the bush was burning and burning, but it did not burn up! He walked toward the bush to see if he could figure out what was going on.

"Moses! Moses!" the Lord called to him.

"Here I am," Moses answered.

"Don't come any closer," the Lord said. "Take your sandals off because this is holy ground." Then He said, "I am the God of your ancestors Abraham, Isaac, and Jacob."

When Moses heard this, he was terrified. He hid his face in his hands because he was afraid to look at God.

"Moses," God said, "I have seen the misery of my people in Egypt. I've heard their cries to be free from the slavery of the Egyptians. I know they have been suffering and I am going to rescue them. I am going to lead them out of Egypt and to their own land. It is the land of Canaan—a wonderful land flowing with milk and honey. Yes, the cries of the people have been heard. Moses, I am sending you to talk to Pharaoh. You will lead my people out of Egypt."

"Wait," Moses said, "Who am I to talk to Pharaoh? How can you expect me to lead the Israelites out of Egypt?"

"Don't worry," God said, "I will be with you. Bring the people out of Egypt then return right to this mountain and worship me."

"But if I go to the people and tell them that God instructed me to lead them out of Egypt they won't believe me. They will ask what Your name is. What should I tell them?"

"Tell them that I AM has sent you to them. Now go call the leaders of the Israelites together. Tell them that God appeared to you in a burning bush. Tell them that I promise to rescue them from Egypt and lead them to their own land."

Moses wasn't sure that the Israelites would listen to him. So God told him to throw his shepherd's staff down on the ground. When Moses did, God made it turn into a snake. Then God told Moses to pick up the snake. When he did, it turned back into a staff. That showed Moses God's power! "Do this for the people and they will listen to you," God said. Moses still thought the people wouldn't listen to him, so God gave him a few other ways Moses could help them believe. But then Moses said he wasn't sure that he could do what God was asking him to do because he wasn't good at speaking in public. God got a little angry with Moses but He agreed to let Moses' brother, Aaron, go with him. God would speak to Moses. Moses would tell Aaron what God said, then Aaron would speak to Pharaoh and the people.

The Plagues on Egypt *Exodus 7:14–10:29*

Moses and Aaron went to the Egyptian Pharaoh and told him, "The Lord God says, 'Let my people go so they can worship me in the wilderness.'" Pharaoh refused to listen to them. He didn't care at all what their God said. It was time for a more direct approach. God told Moses and Aaron to go back to Pharaoh. "Meet him on the banks of the river. Take along your shepherd's staff. Tell Pharaoh that I say he should let my people go! If he refuses again, hit the waters of the river with your staff. I will turn the water to blood. All the water in Egypt will be blood but the water where you Israelites live will be just fine." God was right; the water turned to blood. But that didn't convince Pharaoh to let the Israelites go.

God sent a second plague on the Egyptian people. He made thousands and thousands of frogs fill the land of Egypt. There were frogs everywhere. The Egyptians couldn't take a step without squishing a frog. But there were no frogs where the Israelites lived. Still Pharaoh would not let the people go.

God wasn't finished with Pharaoh. The third plague happened when Aaron hit the dusty earth with his staff and all the dust turned into gnats. The little bugs flew into mouths, ears, eyes—they were everywhere—except where the Israelites lived. Pharaoh still would not let the people go.

The next plague sent on the Egyptians was flies. Flies were all around. The Egyptian people couldn't take a bite of food without getting flies in their mouths. Still Pharaoh said that the Israelites could not leave.

The fifth plague was against all the livestock the Egyptians owned. Their horses, cows, donkeys, camels, and sheep died. The Israelites' animals were fine. Still Pharaoh would not let God's people leave Egypt.

During the sixth plague, the Egyptians' bodies were covered with painful boils. The people were miserable but Pharaoh would not release the Israelites.

Crops were destroyed with the next plague. Hail crashed down on the Egyptians' fields. The eighth plague was on the crops too. Locusts came and ate everything that the hail hadn't destroyed in the fields. Pharaoh still refused to let the Israelites leave.

The ninth plague was darkness. For three days it was so dark that the Egyptians could not even see where they were going. By now the Egyptian people were ready for Pharaoh to send the Israelites out of Egypt but Pharaoh still refused.

God had one more plague to send. It would finally convince the Pharaoh to listen to God and release God's people from slavery.

The Last Plague and God's Deliverance
Exodus 11, 12

God sent nine plagues on the Egyptian people to try to convince Pharaoh to let the Israelites out of slavery. God wanted His people free. But even though the nine plagues were terrible, Pharaoh refused to let the people go. God had one more plague to send. He was sure this one would convince Pharaoh because it was awful. God would pass through the land of Egypt and the firstborn son of every family would die, including the oldest son of Pharaoh. Even the firstborn of the animals would die. The Israelites would not be protected from this plague unless they did what God told them to do. His instruction was that each household should kill a lamb and smear its blood on the doorpost of their homes. When God passed through the land and saw the blood on their doorposts He promised He would pass over their homes and spare their firstborn children and animals. God also said they should have their households packed up and be ready to go when He told them to leave Egypt. God told the people to remember this day of Passover forever as the day that God protected them.

The Israelites packed their things. They killed the lambs and smeared the blood on the doorposts of their homes and they ate the roasted lambs as they were instructed to do. They even asked the Egyptians to give them gold and silver because God told them to do it and the Egyptians gave it to them. The people did everything God told them to do.

At midnight the Lord moved through the land of Egypt. He killed the firstborn son of every family except where He saw the blood of the lamb on the doorposts. Even the son of Pharaoh died. The land of Egypt was filled with the heartbroken cries of families who had lost their sons.

Pharaoh sent for Moses and Aaron during the night. "Get out!" he cried. "Leave Egypt—you and all your people!" All the people of Egypt begged for the Israelites to leave. So Moses led thousands and thousands of Israelites out of Egypt to the land of Canaan which God had promised to them.

Crossing the Red Sea *Exodus 13:17—14:31*

Pharaoh let the Israelites leave Egypt after the tenth plague. In fact that last plague was so terrible that the Egyptians could not wait for them to leave. Moses led thousands of Israelites as they left Egypt. God's presence was with them the whole way. If anyone ever felt afraid that maybe God had left them, all they had to do was look up. In the daytime a tall column of cloud led them, and at night the column turned to a fire. The Israelites followed this column because they knew it was God's presence. They followed it day and night until God told them to stop and camp. Their camp was right on the shoreline of the Red Sea. That's when they discovered that Pharaoh had changed his mind about letting them leave. He got into his chariot and commanded his soldiers and all the chariots in his army to catch the Israelites and bring them back to Egypt. He didn't want to lose all his slaves. As Pharaoh and his army approached their camp, the Israelites started to panic. They backed up as far as they could, but they were on the shores of the sea. The army was behind them and the sea was in front of them. They were trapped!

The Israelites were terrified and they focused their fear at Moses. "Why did you take us out of Egypt?" they screamed at him. "We were safe there. We are just going to die out here in the wilderness. Slavery in Egypt was better than dying out here!"

Moses tried to calm the people down. "Don't be afraid," he said. "Just wait and see what God is going to do to protect you!" The angel of the Lord moved the column of cloud around behind the Israelites so the Egyptians couldn't see them. Then God told Moses to hold his shepherd's staff out over the Red Sea. When he did, a powerful wind blew up and moved the waters of the sea. The water swished and swirled as it divided into two large walls of water with dry ground between them. "Move," Moses told the Israelites. They began to cross the Red Sea on dry land with walls of water on either side of them. It took all night to cross the sea. The column of cloud turned to fire to lead the people across but still the Egyptians couldn't see them.

As the last Israelite walked out of the sea, the Egyptian chariots and army entered on the other side. They thought they could rush in and capture the Israelites. God saw what they were trying to do so He made the wheels of their chariots fall off and He threw the soldiers

into confusion so they were running into each other or running the wrong way. Then God told Moses to take his hand down and when he did the water of the Red Sea began to crash back together into its normal place. Every chariot was covered by water. The entire Egyptian army drowned that day in the Red Sea but every single Israelite safely reached the other side of the sea.

Food from Heaven *Exodus 16*

After God miraculously led the Israelites through the Red Sea and saved them from the Egyptians, they kept traveling through the wilderness. Day after day, week after week, they walked and walked. Before long the little food they had brought along from Egypt was gone. The people were tired and hungry and even though God had done amazing miracles to free

them from slavery and save them from the Egyptian army, they started complaining and whining. "Moses, why did you even take us out of Egypt? At least we had food there. We're going to starve to death out here in the wilderness."

God heard the people's complaints and He spoke to Moses. "I'm going to send food down from Heaven for the people. They can go out each day and pick up all the food they need for that day. However, I'm going to give them

a little test to see if they will follow my instructions. Tell the people to pick up only what they need for their families each day except on the sixth day when they should pick up twice what they need. No food will come on the seventh day."

Moses called all the people together and said, "Every night you will have proof that it was God himself who led you out of Egypt. Every morning you will see proof of His presence with you. He has heard your complaining, which is against Him, not against Aaron or me. God promises to give you meat to eat every evening and bread every morning. This is His promise to you."

That very evening hundreds and hundreds of quail flew into the camp and landed on the ground. The people could capture them without even trying very hard. The next morning when the people got up the ground was wet with dew. As the dew dried up, thin white flakes were left on the ground. The Israelites were confused. "What is this?" they asked.

Moses answered, "It is the bread God promised you. Here is His instruction: 'Pick up only what you need for your family for this day.'" It would be about two quarts for each person. By obeying God's instructions each person had just enough to eat. But Moses warned the people, "Do not try to pick up extra to keep overnight." Of course some people tried to do that, but by the next morning it was rotted, full of bugs, and very, very stinky.

Every day the people picked up what they needed and any flakes left on the ground melted away in the sun. On the sixth day there was extra manna (that's what the flakes were called) so the people picked up enough to last them for two days. That's what God told them to do because the seventh day was to be a day of rest. The manna was sweet and tasted like honey cakes. Between the quail and the manna, the people had plenty of food to eat. God sent manna six days a week for 40 years—until the people were settled in the land of Canaan where they could grow their own crops.

Water from a Rock *Exodus 17:1-7*

A little while after God began sending manna and quail to the people, He told them to break camp and start walking again. They still needed to get to the land God had promised to give them. The people traveled as far as a place called Rephidim but there was no water there. Right away the people started complaining to Moses, "Give us water to drink! Why did you take us out of Egypt? We had plenty of water there. We're all going to die out here with no water to drink!" Moses tried to remind them of all the miracles God had already done to take care of them. But they just wanted to complain.

"Quiet!" Moses cried. "Why are you arguing with me? Why are you complaining against God?"

The people kept complaining so Moses turned to God and asked, "What do I do with these people? They are going to come after me with stones!"

God said, "Take your shepherd's staff; the same one that you used when you struck the waters of the Nile River and I turned them to blood. Call the leaders of the people to come with you and walk on ahead of the people. I will meet with you by a large rock near Mt. Sinai. Hit the rock with your staff and I will make water pour out of it. The people will be able to drink as much water as they want. Then they will stop complaining."

Moses did what God told him to do and the people had all the water they wanted. Moses named that place *Massah* which means "the place of testing" and *Meribah* which means "the place of arguing" because the people argued with Moses by asking whether or not God was going to take care of them.

The Ten Commandments *Exodus 20*

It had been two months since the Israelites left Egypt. After they left Rephidim, the place where water came from a rock, God called Moses to come up to the top of Mt. Sinai. He wanted to talk to Moses alone because He had special instructions for the people about how they should live. God wanted Moses to take the instructions to the people and get

their commitments to live by these instructions. The people were not allowed to go up the mountain with Moses or even get close to the mountain.

The instructions that God gave Moses are called the Ten Commandments.

They are:

1. Do not worship any other gods besides God.

2. Do not make any idols to worship because God is a jealous God and won't share your worship.

3. Do not use the name of the Lord your God in a bad way. You will be punished if you do.

4. Keep the Sabbath holy. You can work six days a week, but rest on the seventh day.

5. Honor your father and mother, then you will live a long life.

6. Do not murder.

7. Do not commit adultery.

8. Do not steal.

9. Do not lie about your neighbor.

10. Do not want what your neighbor has.

God delivered these instructions to Moses in a crash of thunder and the loud blast of a horn. Smoke and lightning billowed from the mountain and the people were very afraid. God wrote them on stone tablets with His own hand. Moses took the tablets down to the people and told them what God's instructions were. The people agreed to live by these rules.

The Golden Calf *Exodus 32*

God called Moses to come up on Mt. Sinai for a private meeting. Moses left Aaron in charge of the people. Moses was gone for a long time. In fact he was gone so long that the people didn't think he was going to come back at all. So they went to Aaron and said, "We need a god who can lead us. Moses has disappeared and we don't think he is even coming back. Make a god for us!"

Aaron said, "OK, everyone take off any gold jewelry you are wearing and bring it to me." All the people obeyed Aaron and he soon had a large pile of gold jewelry in front of him. Aaron put the gold in a pot and melted it down to liquid. Then he molded and formed

the liquid gold into the shape of a calf. When the people saw it they cheered and cried, "This is the god who brought us out of Egypt." Aaron saw how excited the people were about the golden calf and how popular he was for making it. He built an altar and announced that the next day there would be a festival in honor of the Lord.

The people were very excited and they got up early to sacrifice burnt offerings and peace offerings. They celebrated with feasts and drinking and many kinds of behaviors that did not please God.

Meanwhile, up on Mt. Sinai, God knew what was going on with the people. "Moses, go back down the mountain to your people. They have done something terrible. They agreed to live by my Ten Commandments but they are already disobeying me. They have made an idol that looks like a golden calf and are worshiping it and making sacrifices to it. They are saying that this god is who brought them out of Egypt. Moses, leave me alone now so that my anger can rage against these people. I will destroy all of them and I will make you, Moses, into a great nation!"

Moses couldn't believe what the people had done. He was angry and disappointed too, but he begged God to spare the people. "O God," he said, "You brought these people out of Egypt. You have done miracles to save them and You said that You would make their descendants as many as there are stars in the sky. O God, You promised to give the land of Canaan to these people. Please God, remember Your covenant with these people."

So God took back His threat to destroy the people. Moses went down the mountain, carrying the two stone tablets with the instructions for how the people should live. When he got to the camp he saw the calf and saw the people dancing. He threw the tablets to the ground in anger and they broke into pieces.

Moses took the golden calf, melted it in a fire, and then ground the gold into powder. He mixed the powder with water and made the people drink it. Then he turned to Aaron and asked, "What were you thinking? Why did you do this?"

"Don't get so upset. I just threw their gold jewelry into the fire and this calf is what came out," Aaron lied.

Moses saw that the people were disobedient so he said, "Any of you who are on the Lord's side with me, come stand over here!" The whole tribe of Levi came and from that day on they were the tribe who served God.

The Twelve Spies *Numbers 13*

The Israelites had walked and walked as God led them through the wilderness to the land of Canaan. It was the land He promised to give to them when He had Moses lead them out of Egypt. As the whole nation of Israel camped at the edge of the land of Canaan, God told Moses to send some men into Canaan to explore it and report back. So Moses chose one man from each of the 12 tribes of Israel. He told them to go into Canaan and explore the land. He especially wanted to know about the

people who lived there. He wanted to know if they were tall or if they looked very strong. It was important to know if there were many people in the land or only a few. The spies should find out if the soil was healthy and grew good crops and they should also see what kinds of crops and fruits grew there. God told Moses to have the spies find out everything they could about the land of Canaan. So the spies sneaked into the land and then explored it. They came to one place where grapes grew and the spies cut down a huge cluster of big, juicy grapes to take back and show Moses. They took samples of other kinds of fruits they found too.

The spies searched out the land for 40 days and then returned to Moses to give their reports. The entire nation of Israel gathered to hear what the spies had to say about the land of Canaan. They showed the fruit they had gathered. They told Moses and the people, "The land of Canaan is magnificent. The soil is healthy and it grows big and healthy crops like we've never seen before. But the people living there are like giants."

Ten of the spies said, "We felt like grasshoppers next to the people of Canaan. They are strong and powerful. The cities have strong walls around them. There is no way that we could take this land because the cities are protected and the people more powerful than we are."

But two spies, Joshua and Caleb, said, "Yes, the people of Canaan are big and strong. Yes, there are many of them, but we can win against them. After all, we have God on our side. Come on, people, and be courageous. We can do it!" However, even though the people had seen God do many amazing miracles for them, they listened to the 10 frightened spies instead of the two courageous spies. They refused to try to take the land of Canaan.

God was not pleased that the Israelites did not trust Him. He said that the present generation of Israelites would die before the nation was ever allowed to enter the promised land. The whole nation would wander in the wilderness for 40 years. Only Joshua and Caleb, the two hopeful spies, would be allowed to enter the promised land.

The Bronze Serpent *Numbers 21:4-9*

As the people of Israel wandered through the wilderness—because of their punishment for not trusting God and taking the land when God first led them there—they were once more near the Red Sea. The people got impatient with the roundabout route they were taking. They were tired of walking and just wanted to be in the land. They started complaining against Moses and Aaron once again. "Why have you led us out here to the wilderness to die?" they cried. "Why didn't you just leave us alone in Egypt?" Never mind that they were slaves in Egypt! "There is nothing to eat here. We don't have anything to drink either! We are sick to death of this manna too!"

God was tired of the complaining. He was sad that the people kept forgetting all the miracles He had done for them.

So He sent poisonous snakes slithering among the people. Many people were bitten and some of them died. The people immediately came to Moses and cried, "We've sinned! We're sorry that we spoke against God and against you. Please, pray that God will forgive us. Ask Him to take away the snakes!" Moses listened and prayed for the people.

So God told Moses to make a snake out of bronze. It should look just like the snakes that were biting and killing the people. "Attach the bronze snake to a pole and post it among the people. Anyone who is bitten by the snakes but looks at the bronze snake you have made will be saved." Moses did what God told him to do. The people who looked at the bronze snake, as God instructed, were healed from the snake bites.

THE STORY OF JOSHUA

Moses led God's people out of Egypt just as God asked him to do. It wasn't easy because every time something went wrong or took longer than they thought it should, the people turned on Moses and complained and whined. One time Moses' patience with the people was completely gone and when God told him what to do, Moses disobeyed. Because of his disobedience, Moses was not allowed to enter the promised land. For 40 years Moses led the people to the promised land, but he never got to step inside it. God did, however, let Moses see the land. A new leader was chosen to lead the Israelites into the promised land. His name was Joshua.

A New Leader *Deuteronomy 31:1-8*

When Moses was 120 years old, God told him it was time for him to step aside as the leader of the Israelites. God also told Moses, "I will cross over the Jordan ahead of the people. I will destroy the people and nations living there and help your people take possession of the land."

The Israelites waited expectantly to hear if God would appoint a new leader or if they would choose their own. God had already made a decision. Joshua would be the new leader of the Israelite nation. Moses announced that Joshua was his replacement. He said that God promised them that Joshua would lead them. "Be brave and strong," Moses commanded the people, "because God is with you. He will never fail you!"

Moses called Joshua to come up in front of all the people. "Joshua, God has chosen you to be the new leader of these people. Be strong and courageous because you will lead these people into the land God promised to give their ancestors. You are the one who will lead them into the fulfillment of that promise. God is with you. He will always be with you."

Soon after that, Moses went to Mount Nebo and climbed up to the top. God let Moses see the whole promised land. "This is the land I promised to Abraham, Isaac, and Jacob," God said. "I promised I would give it to their descendants. I'm allowing you to see it, but you cannot enter it." Moses died up on that mountain and no one knows where his body is buried.

Joshua took over leadership of the Israelites. The people listened to him and obeyed him. They knew that God had appointed him and that God would be with Joshua as he led them. God had one strong commandment for Joshua, "Obey all the laws that Moses gave you. Study the Book of the Law continually. Think about it day and night so that you will know when you are obeying or disobeying it. Only by obeying it will you succeed."

A Woman Named Rahab *Joshua 2*

od's first job for Joshua was to actually bring the people into the promised land. They had been moving toward that for 40 long years. The city of Jericho was the first place God wanted them to capture so Joshua sent two spies into that city to check things out. They crept into the city, thinking no one noticed them, and they went to the home of a woman named Rahab. She did not serve God. Some people did see the two spies sneak into Jericho and those people hurried to tell the king about them. The king immediately sent a message to Rahab, "Bring those two men out who are hiding in your house because they are spies sent here by our enemies to check out our city."

But Rahab had already thought that the king might ask this so she had hidden the spies on her rooftop. She sent this message back to him, "Yes, those two men were here but I didn't realize they were spies. As the city gate was being closed at sunset, they left the city. I don't know where they went but if you send your soldiers out quickly, you may find them." Actually, Rahab had hidden the spies beneath some stalks of flax that were on her rooftop. Even if the king's men had gone up to the roof, they would not have seen the spies. Instead, though, the king's men rushed through the city gates and went to search for the two spies.

After the king's men left, Rahab went back up to the roof to talk with the spies. "I know your God has given you this land. I know you will capture this city. The residents of Jericho are terrified of you. We've heard how your God parted the Red Sea to get your people through it and then crashed the waters down on the Egyptian army. All of our hearts shook with fear when we heard that and other stories of how He protected you. I'm asking you to show kindness and protection to me and my family since I have protected you. When you capture this city will you spare our lives? Give me a sign so that I know I can trust you."

"We will honor your kindness to us," the spies promised. "We will make sure you and your family are spared."

Rahab used a rope to let the men down over the city wall through her window. "Run into the nearby hills and hide for three days," she told them. By then the king's men would stop searching for them and it would be safe for them to go back to Joshua and the rest of the Israelites.

Before they left, the spies said, "Hang a red cord in your window so

that we will know which house is yours when we come to take Jericho. If you don't do that, our promise to spare you does not stand. If any of your family leaves the house and goes out into the street when we are taking the city, we cannot promise their safety."

Rahab agreed and hung the red cord in her window right away. The spies hid in the hills for three days then returned to Joshua to report on the city. They said, "We can take the city of Jericho. God has promised it to us and the people there are afraid of us because of Him."

The Fall of Jericho *Joshua 3, 4, 6*

The first step to capturing Jericho was to cross over the Jordan River. However, it was at flood stage, so how would the people get across? God told Joshua exactly what to do. He had the priests carry the ark of the covenant into the edge of the river's waters. The people watched and waited as they did that. When their feet touched the water, the river water

backed up into a pile and made a dry space for the Israelites to cross. The priests stood there until every Israelite had crossed the riverbed. Then they brought the ark of the covenant out of the river and the waters crashed back into place at flood stage as before. Joshua had leaders from the 12 tribes set up stones on the shore of the river as an altar of praise for God protecting them.

When the Israelites reached Jericho, it was shut up tight. The gates were locked and there was no sign of life inside the walls. God assured Joshua that the city would fall to his army. He gave Joshua specific instructions on how to approach the battle. "March all the way around the city walls once a day with all your soldiers. Do this for six days," God said. "This is the order you should march in: The armed soldiers lead the group and then seven priests each carrying a trumpet are next. Behind them is the ark of the covenant and another guard unit is behind it. The priests should blow their horns as you march, but the people must be completely quiet."

Joshua explained the plan to the people and emphasized, "You've got to be completely quiet until I give you the sign, then you shout for all you're worth!" They marched once a day for six days. The people inside Jericho must have wondered what they were up to. On the seventh day Joshua's people marched around the city seven times, just as God instructed. On the seventh time around, Joshua gave a sign and all the people shouted! When they did the great walls of Jericho crumbled and fell down. Joshua's soldiers climbed over the fallen walls and ran in to capture the city. The two spies remembered to look for the red cord in Rahab's window. They found it and led her and her family to safety just as they promised they would. Rahab stayed with the Israelites for the rest of her life.

From that time on none of the people questioned Joshua's leadership of their nation.

The Sun Stands Still *Joshua 10:1-15*

J oshua and the Israelites set up camp near the people of Gibeon. Joshua and the king of Gibeon made an agreement that their people would live in peace with one an- other. That was fine until the king of Jerusalem realized that the Gibeonites and Israelites were friends. He was wor- ried that the two nations might get to- gether and declare war on his people.

So the king of Jerusalem got four other kings of nearby nations to join him in declaring war on Gibeon. They thought they would beat the Gibeonites at their own plan.

As soon as the five nations attacked, the king of Gibeon sent an urgent message to Joshua. "Help us!" he cried. "Don't desert us now when these five armies are attacking us. Help!" Joshua didn't ignore him. He marched his army right up to where the battle was raging.

God told Joshua, "Don't be afraid of them. I am delivering these five nations into your hands. You will win and not one of them will be left standing!"

It took all night for Joshua's army to reach the battlefield but when they did they took their enemies by surprise. The Lord made the enemy soldiers confused so they didn't know what they were doing and Joshua's army easily defeated them. His army chased the soldiers away and as they were running God sent a hailstorm on them. The large hailstones killed more of the enemy soldiers than Joshua's soldiers did.

During the battle that day Joshua stood before all the Israelites and said to God, "Make the sun stand still. Hold back the moon so that we can have complete victory today!" God did it! He made the sun stop in the middle of the sky and stand still for a full day! There has never been another day like that. Everyone knew that God was fighting for Israel.

THE TIME OF THE JUDGES

When Joshua died, a new form of leadership was put in place for the nation of Israel. A series of judges were empowered and strengthened by God to lead the nation. Sometimes the people obeyed God and sometimes they did not. God used women as well as men as leaders of the people. The people had to learn a few lessons over and over: to let God lead them, to serve only God, that sin is wrong, and that they had to confess their sins.

Judge Deborah *Judges 4*

The people of Israel stopped obeying God. They were sinning and living selfish lives. So God made them slaves of King Jabin of Canaan. For 20 years, the commander of Jabin's army, Sisera, was mean to the Israelites.

Deborah was the prophetess judge of Israel at that time. She sat under a palm tree and held court. The Israelites came to her with their problems and had her settle their disputes. The people had been crying out to God to save them from the cruelty of Sisera. God told Deborah to send for a man named Barak because He had a job for him to do. "The God of Israel commands you to take 10,000 men and go to Mount Tabor. He will make Sisera come to you there with all his chariots and soldiers. You will defeat him by God's power."

But Barak said, "I won't go, Deborah, unless you go with me. If you don't go, I won't go."

"Well, OK," Deborah said. "I will go but that means that the honor of killing Sisera will not go to you. It will go to a woman instead." Deborah went with Barak to Mount Tabor. God brought Sisera there with his chariots and soldiers. "Go," Deborah told Barak. "God has brought Sisera here. He's going to deliver him into your hands!"

Barak and 10,000 men headed to where Sisera was camped. When Sisera saw them coming, he took off running, even abandoning his soldiers and chariots. All his soldiers were killed that day; not one man was left. Sisera ran to the tent of a woman named Jael. She told him to come inside her tent. "Come on in. Don't be afraid."

Sisera came in and said, "I'm thirsty. Please give me some water." So Jael gave him a drink and then put a blanket over him so no one would see him. "Don't tell anyone I'm here," Sisera told her.

Jael agreed to protect him but she waited until Sisera had fallen asleep, then she took his life.

Barak arrived soon after that. He had chased Sisera all the way to Jael's tent. Jael took him inside her tent and showed him that Sisera was dead. Jael, a woman, killed Sisera, just as Deborah had said. After that the king of Canaan got weaker and weaker until the Israelites destroyed him.

Gideon *Judges 6, 7*

The Israelites just didn't seem to be able to consistently obey God. After Deborah and Jael had helped free them from Sisera's cruelty they began disobeying God. God let them become slaves again. This time the Midianite people were the slavemasters. For seven years the people cried out to God to rescue them. He heard their prayers and spoke to a man named Gideon. "The Lord is with you, Gideon. You will rescue my people." Gideon didn't immediately believe that he could do want God wanted him to do.

"I need proof that You will use me to save Israel from the Midianites," Gideon said. "I'll put a piece of wool on the ground tonight. If it is wet in the morning but the ground all around is dry, then I'll believe You." That's exactly what happened, but it wasn't good enough for Gideon. "Don't be angry with me but show me once again. This time make the wool dry and the ground around it covered with water." God did that for him.

Gideon finally believed that God wanted to use him to free the Israelites so he called all his men together. He had about 32,000 men. "You have too many men," God said. "Send home any man who is afraid." About 22,000 men left so Gideon now had an army of 10,000. But God said, "You still have too many men. I want the people to know that it is I who will deliver them, not a big army. Take them down to the water to get a drink. The ones who lap up the water like a dog can stay. The others must leave." That left Gideon with an army of 300 men.

Gideon divided the men into three groups and assigned them places around the Midianite camp. Each man had a trumpet, an empty jar, and a torch.

"Watch me," Gideon said. "When I get to the edge of the enemy camp, do exactly what I do. We will blow our trumpets and shout, 'For the Lord and for Gideon!'"

Gideon waited to blow his trumpet until the Midianites were changing the

guards who watched the camp. All 300 soldiers blew their trumpets and broke the jars that covered the torches they carried. So the Midianites thought they were surrounded by many more than just 300 men. They got confused and began fighting each other and eventually all ran away. Gideon's little army of 300 men defeated the much bigger Midianite army because God fought for them.

Samson's Victory *Judges 13, 16*

The Israelites disobeyed God again. After Gideon's army won their freedom, the people did evil in God's sight. So, once again, God let them become slaves. This time they became slaves to the Philistines and it lasted 40 years. During this time an Israelite man and woman who had not been able to have children had a baby boy. The boy was to be a Nazirite, one who is set apart to serve God from birth. This boy would be the one God used to deliver the people from slavery to the Philistines. His name was

Samson and as he grew up his hair was never cut because that was a sign of his obedience to God.

Samson didn't always make wise choices though. He married a Philistine woman. He made the Philistine people really angry with him by tricking them with a riddle. Then, when they tried to get even with him, he murdered many of them. He was so strong and powerful that no one had a chance against him; in fact, he was the strongest man in the world! The Philistines became sworn enemies of Samson. They knew that the best way to capture him was to get a woman to trick him because he couldn't say no to a pretty girl. They got a woman named Delilah to trick Samson into telling her why he was so strong. He tried to lie to her, but finally admitted that if his hair was cut he would be as weak as any other man. Delilah waited until he fell asleep then called in the Philistines to cut Samson's hair and capture him. They didn't just capture him though; they gouged out his eyes so he couldn't see a thing. They really hated him.

Samson was kept in prison until a special Philistine celebration. They brought him out that day to parade him around and celebrate that he could no longer hurt them. The Philistines enjoyed making fun of him. What they didn't realize was that the whole time they had him in prison, Samson's hair was growing long again and his heart desired again to serve God completely. When they were tired of making fun of Samson, they chained him to a column

of the great hall where they were celebrating. "Please God," Samson prayed, "Help me to defeat these Philistines, Your enemies. Give me the strength that I need once more." God heard Samson's prayer and He answered it.

The Philistines went on with their celebrating and paid little attention to Samson. He stepped up between two pillars and felt around until he could place one hand on each pillar. "God help me," he prayed again. Then he began pushing against the pillars with all his strength. He pushed and pushed and slowly the two pillars cracked, then crumbled down. The great hall collapsed, killing all the Philistines who were inside it. Samson died that day too but he killed more Philistines that day than he had in his whole life.

THE STORY OF RUTH

From the time that Adam and Eve first sinned, God had a plan for a way to bring people back to himself. He had a plan for the birth of the Messiah. During the time of the judges of Israel, God continued working out His plan for the birth of His Son. The ancestral line through which Jesus would be born was very important. The gentle story of the loyal woman named Ruth tells the next step toward the birth of the Messiah. Her story is one of a woman who knew what she wanted and reached for it.

A Loyal Woman *The Book of Ruth*

A famine settled over the land of Judah. There was no food and people were starving to death. A man named Elimelech and his wife, Naomi, couldn't stand the thought that their two sons would die so they left Judah and moved to the land of Moab where there was plenty of food. Naomi relaxed a little with the stress of how to feed her family gone. But then, her husband Elimelech suddenly died. Her two sons married girls from Moab but then the two young men suddenly died too. Naomi was left in Moab with her two Moabite daughters-in-law. Naomi was lonely for her family and heard that the famine in Judah was over so she decided to return to her homeland. Naomi's two daughters-in-law said that they wanted to go to Judah with her. But Naomi suggested that they might want to

go back to their families and hope for new husbands. After all, they were still young women. One daughter-in-law, Orpah, decided to return home. But the other one, Ruth, insisted that she wanted to go with Naomi. "I want to go wherever you go," she said. "Your people will be my people and your God will be my God." Ruth was determined so Naomi allowed her to come with her to the town of Bethlehem. They settled there and Ruth looked for a way to provide food for herself and her mother-in-law. "I have a relative named Boaz who owns some fields," Naomi told Ruth.

"I will go to his fields and pick up any leftover grain for us to use to make bread," Ruth said. She went day after day

to pick up bits of grain. Boaz saw her there and asked someone who she was. The person told him that she was the daughter-in-law of his relative, Naomi.

"Leave extra grain for her," Boaz instructed. He appreciated how hard-working she was and that she took good care of Naomi.

Ruth noticed Boaz too. She thought he was a nice man. They talked one day and he gave Ruth lots of extra grain to take back to Naomi. Boaz did many nice things for Ruth. They eventually got married and took Naomi into their home too. Boaz and Ruth had a baby whom they named Obed. When Obed grew up he had a son named Jesse. When Jesse grew up he had a son named David. These men were all ancestors of Jesus, the Son of God.

GOD'S SERVANT, SAMUEL

The last judge in Israel's history was named Samuel. While Samuel was judge the people of Israel insisted on having a king like the countries around them. Samuel tried to tell them that God said it wasn't a good idea, but they wouldn't have it any other way. From boyhood Samuel tried to serve God. He made mistakes, but in his heart Samuel always longed to obey God. Samuel's life intertwined with Saul's life, the first king of Israel, and David, a future king and a man whom God called, "a man after God's own heart."

Young Samuel *1 Samuel 1; 3:1-21*

Elkanah made a special trip to Shiloh each year to worship God. He had two wives, Peninnah and Hannah. He loved Hannah the most but she did not have any children. Peninnah had children and she made fun of Hannah for being childless. One year Elkanah brought his two wives to Shiloh to worship God. Hannah's heart was breaking because she really wanted to have a child. One night she went by herself to the tabernacle to ask God to give her a child. Hannah fell to her knees and cried very hard. In her heart she was praying; in fact her mouth moved with prayer but she said no words aloud. "God, please, in Your mercy, give me a son. I promise You that I will give him back to You to be Your servant!"

An old priest, Eli, watched the woman crying and apparently talking to herself. He didn't know she was praying. He thought she was drunk. "Woman," he said, "why do you come in here after you've been drinking?"

"No, sir! I'm not drunk," Hannah cried. "I was asking God to give me a son. I promised to give my son back to Him to be His servant. Oh, sir, my heart aches to be a mother."

"Well," Eli said, "may God grant your request."

Less than a year later, Hannah did have a baby boy and she named him Samuel. When the little boy was old enough to live away from his family she took Samuel back to the tabernacle to live. Eli, the priest, taught Samuel how to serve God.

One night young Samuel went to bed in the tabernacle. He was tired from a long day of work. Just as he was about to fall asleep he heard, "Samuel! Samuel!" He quickly got up and ran to where Eli was sleeping.

"Here I am. What do you need?" Samuel asked. But Eli answered that he didn't call for Samuel and he told the little boy to go back to bed.

Samuel crawled back into bed but soon heard his name called again. Once again he ran to Eli. But, once again, Eli told the young boy that he had not called him and he sent him back to bed.

So for a third time Samuel went to bed. Again he heard the voice call, "Samuel!" So once again he ran to Eli and asked

what the old priest wanted.

By now Eli knew that it was God calling for Samuel. "When your name is called again answer with, 'Here I am, Lord. I'm listening.'" Samuel did what Eli suggested and God told him what some of His future plans were. As Samuel grew up, God was always with him helping him be wise and helpful to many people.

THE FIRST KING OF ISRAEL

One of the problems that the Israelite people kept having was that they looked at the nations around them and wanted the same things those nations had. What they didn't realize was that they didn't need those things because they had God! That was certainly the case when the Israelites started clamoring to have a king like the nations around them. God's servant, Samuel, tried to tell the people that they didn't need a king because they had God and His priests, but the people wouldn't listen. God chose to give the people what they wanted, and He chose the man who would become the first king of Israel.

King Saul *1 Samuel 9; 10:1, 17-26*

A rich man named Kish had a son named Saul who was tall and handsome. One day some of Kish's donkeys wandered away and Kish sent Saul and a servant to look for them. They couldn't find the donkeys anywhere so they decided to ask for help from a man of God they had heard about.

At the same time God spoke to Samuel about the man He had chosen to become the first king of Israel. He told Samuel he would point out this man to him. So, when Saul and his servant approached Samuel about helping them find the missing donkeys, God said to Samuel, "This is the man I told you about. He will be king of Israel." Of course, Saul didn't know about God's plan so he was completely surprised when Samuel asked him to come to a great banquet hall for dinner and then seated him at a place of honor. Saul was given the best dinner and then taken to Samuel's house to rest for the night. The next morning Samuel told him, "I have been given a special message from God about you. He has chosen you to be the next leader of Israel." Samuel poured a little olive oil over Saul's head, anointing him to be the king.

Sometime later Samuel called all the Israelite people together and gave them a message from God. "I brought you out of Egypt and rescued you many

times from your enemies. Even though I have done so much for you, you still insist on having a king. So divide into your tribes and stand before me." All the tribes stood together and God chose the tribe of Benjamin. Samuel brought each Benjamite before God and finally Saul, son of Kish, came forward. He was the man chosen to become king. Samuel announced that to the people, but when they turned to look for Saul, he was gone!

"Where is he? What happened to him?" the people asked each other.

"He's hiding," God said. They found Saul and brought him out. He was taller than anyone else.

"This is the man God has chosen to be your king," Samuel said.

"Long live the king!" the people shouted. God sent a group of men who loved Him to be Saul's assistants. But there were a few evil men of Israel who didn't like Saul and refused to follow him.

A Change in Leadership

1 Samuel 13:7-14; 15:1-23

S aul was God's choice to be the first king of Israel, but Saul didn't always make good decisions. One time when Israel was at war with the Philistines, the battle got ugly and the men of Israel ran away. Saul and his own men were hiding at a place called Gilgal, trembling with fear. They waited there for seven days for Samuel to arrive. He told Saul earlier to wait for him there. Saul's soldiers were so scared of the Philistines that they were running away, one at a time. So Saul took matters into his own hands and

offered a burnt sacrifice himself. Just as he finished, Samuel arrived. "What are you doing?" Samuel asked.

"Well, my men were afraid and some of them ran away. I was trying to stop them. I know that the Philistines are ready to go to battle with us but we can't fight if we haven't asked for God's help. You weren't here so I had to do it myself."

"You have disobeyed God's command. If you had obeyed, God would have made you king of Israel forever. But now, your reign must end for God has found a man whose heart follows His. He has already chosen this man to be the new king," Samuel said.

A while later, Saul once again disobeyed God. He was ordered to have his soldiers destroy the Amalekites—all of them. But instead of obeying, Saul captured the king and let his soldiers take a lot of the cattle and sheep. Samuel challenged Saul on his disobedience. But as usual, Saul had an excuse. "Yes, we brought back the best of the sheep and cattle but we're going to use them to make sacrifices to God! And yes, I brought back the king but all the rest of the nation was wiped out."

"You did not obey God," Samuel said firmly.

"But we are going to sacrifice the animals we captured to God. He wants our sacrifices!" Saul said.

"Yes, God wants our sacrifices but He wants our obedience more! What do you think pleases God most? Sacrifices or obedience? It is obedience!" Samuel insisted.

After that, God chose a man who would be the new king of Israel. He was finished with Saul's excuses and disobedience. Samuel would anoint the new king very soon.

The New King of Israel *1 Samuel 16:1-13*

S amuel, I have chosen a new king for Israel," God said. "I want you to go to Bethlehem and meet a man named Jesse. One of his sons will be the new king and I want you to anoint him."

"But God, if King Saul hears that I have had a part in anointing a new king, he will kill me!" Samuel said.

"Just tell him that you are going there to offer a sacrifice. King Saul can't argue with that. Then when you get

there invite Jesse and his sons to come to the sacrifice service."

Samuel did exactly what God said. He announced that he was going to Bethlehem to make a sacrifice to God. When he arrived he found Jesse and invited him and all of his sons to the service. "I will show you which of Jesse's sons is the one I have chosen. Have each of them brought before you, one at a time, and wait for me to tell you which boy will be king."

Jesse called his oldest son, Eliab, to come forward. "This must be the right boy," Samuel thought. After all, Eliab was tall and handsome. He was an impressive young man.

But God stopped Samuel right away. "This is not the one I have chosen. Yes, he looks good on the outside, but I look at people's hearts. What a person is like on the inside is more important to me than how he looks on the outside." So Samuel asked to the next son and the next and the next. None of Jesse's seven sons was the one God had chosen to be king.

"Do you have any other sons?" Samuel asked Jesse.

"Well, the youngest is out in the fields with my sheep," Jesse answered.

"Send for him immediately," Samuel said.

When young David walked into the room, God said, "This is the one. Anoint him to be Israel's next king." Samuel anointed the boy with oil and God's Spirit came on David that day.

David Fights Goliath *1 Samuel 17:1-51*

The Philistines camped near Succoth and declared war on King Saul's army. The two armies camped on opposite hills and faced each other. One Philistine soldier named Goliath was a giant. He was over nine feet tall and wore armor that weighed 125 pounds. Just the head of his spear weighed 15 pounds. A man who carried his armor walked ahead of him wherever he went. Every day Goliath came down the hillside and shouted at King Saul's army. "Hey, do you need a whole army to settle this battle? Choose your best soldier and send him out to fight me. If your man is able to kill me then all the Philistines will be your slaves. But if I kill your man you will become our slaves." Goliath did this twice a day for 40 days. All of King Saul's soldiers were terrified so none of them would fight Goliath.

Jesse's three oldest sons were soldiers in King Saul's army. One day Jesse sent his youngest son, David, to take supplies to his brothers and then asked him to come back and tell him how the three boys were doing. As David came into camp, he heard Goliath shouting at the Israelites. He couldn't understand why none of King Saul's soldiers would go fight him. He was surprised that no one volunteered to go fight the giant.

"Did you see that giant?" they asked. "Did you know that King Saul will give a huge reward to any soldier who kills him? He will even give him one of his daughters to marry." Even with the great reward offered none of the soldiers would volunteer to fight the giant.

David went around the camp asking questions about the giant's challenge. His brothers heard that he was asking questions and they got angry with him. "Go home," they said. "You're supposed to be watching Father's sheep! What are you doing snooping around here?"

David ignored them and went right to King Saul. "Sir, I will fight the giant," he said.

"You? You're just a boy and Goliath has been a soldier all his life!" King Saul said. "You wouldn't have a chance against him."

"No, I can do it," David insisted. "I take care of my father's sheep and defend them against wild animals!"

King Saul thought about it and then said, "OK, but you have to wear my armor to keep you a little safer." David

tried the armor on but it was so heavy he couldn't move. So he took it off. He started down the hillside, stopping to pick up five smooth stones.

Goliath saw the young boy coming out to fight him and he got angry. "What do you think I am, a dog?" he shouted. "Come on, I'll feed you to the birds!"

"You are big and strong. You have a spear and a shield. But I have the strength and power of God himself on my side," David shouted. He put a stone in his slingshot and twirled it over his head. When he let it go, the stone sailed through the air and landed squarely on Goliath's forehead. The giant crashed to the ground and David ran down the hill, grabbed Goliath's sword, and cut off his head! The Philistine army took off running and the Israelites chased them.

The news spread quickly of David's victory over Goliath. The people made up songs about his power. At first everyone loved David, but after a while one person got tired of hearing about him; in fact he became very jealous of young David. That person was King Saul.

Jonathan and David *1 Samuel 18:1-4; 20*

Instead of celebrating young David's victory over the Philistine giant, Goliath, King Saul became very jealous of David. He didn't like the instant popularity David had with the people. David met King Saul's son, Jonathan, and the two became instant friends even though God had chosen David to be the next king of Israel, not Jonathan. In fact, Jonathan made a special pact with David to be his friend forever and gave him his robe, tunic, sword, bow, and belt as a seal to that pact.

Jonathan's friendship was important to David later when King Saul had become so jealous of him that he couldn't stand it. He tried several times to kill David and finally, after one especially close call, David ran away. He talked to Jonathan in secret and asked, "What have I done to make your father want to kill me?" Jonathan couldn't believe that his father really did want David dead. He thought that David must be mistaken. The best friends had to find out how serious King Saul was about killing David, so they came up with a plan.

"Tomorrow is a big festival," David said. "I'll hide in the field and not attend the festival dinner. If your father asks where I am, tell him I went to visit my family. If he just responds with 'fine' then we will know that he doesn't want to harm me. However, if he gets angry then you will know he was planning to murder me. Do this for me, as an honor to our pact to be friends," David pleaded.

"I will do it," Jonathan promised. "I will go to the pile of stones in that field. You hide near there. I will shoot three arrows and then send a servant to get them. If I call to the servant, 'The arrows are on this side,' then you will know that my father is not angry and all is well. However, if I say, 'The arrows are still in front of you,' then you will know that my father does want to harm you and you should never return to our palace."

When the festival dinners came, David was absent two nights in a row. Saul asked where he was and Jonathan told him that he had given David permission to go home and visit his family. King Saul became very angry at his son and even threw a spear at him! It was obvious that he wanted David dead.

Jonathan took a servant boy out to the field and shot his three arrows. As the servant ran to get them, he sadly called out, "No, the arrows are still in front of you!" When the servant left, David came out and the two friends hugged. They were sad to be separated and they promised to be friends forever.

Abigail Shares   *1 Samuel 25*

A fter Samuel died, David and his troop of 400 men camped near a place called Maon. There was a very rich man nearby named Nabal. He had 3,000 sheep and 1,000 goats. His wife was a kind and beautiful woman named Abigail. David heard that Nabal was shearing sheep so he sent 10 of his men to Nabal with a request. "I hear that you are shearing your sheep and I wonder whether you would be so kind as to share some food with us. Remember a

while back when your shepherds were camped near us, we gave them protection and never tried to take anything from them. Would you show us a similar kindness by giving us some food?"

Nabal's response must have surprised David's men. "Why should I share my hard-earned food with a bunch of criminals? I don't know who you are. You may have escaped from your own master. Go away and leave me alone."

David was very angry when he heard what Nabal said. "Get your swords. We're going to fight him," David told his men. Nabal's servants were frightened when they heard that David was planning to attack them.

One servant went to Nabal's wife, Abigail, and told her what was happening. "David and his men were always kind to us. They never harmed us. But now, because of Nabal's mean attitude, there is going to be big trouble for all of us! David is going to kill us all!"

Abigail leaped into action. She called for her servants to load up donkeys with 200 loaves of bread, two skins of wine, five sheep, a bushel of grain, and 300 cakes. She sent her servants ahead

to tell David she was coming with all the food.

When Abigail got close to David, she got off her donkey and bowed low before him. "Please sir, I accept all blame for this problem. Nabal is a mean and wicked man. I did not know your servants came to request food or I would have given them some at once. Please sir, you've never taken vengeance into your own hands and killed for it, please do not start now. Accept this food from me and do not harm Nabal or any of our servants."

David was pleased to hear what Abigail said to him. "Thank you for stopping me from doing wrong. I did plan to kill your husband but because of what you have said I will spare him. Return home and know that all is well."

When Abigail got home she found that Nabal had thrown himself a big party and was celebrating. She waited until the next morning to tell him that David had planned to kill him but she had stopped it. He was so surprised by the news that he had a stroke and died a few days later. When David heard that Nabal was dead, he married Abigail himself.

David Spares Saul *1 Samuel 24, 26*

King Saul was so angry at David that he chased after him. Each time he got close to David he tried to kill him. David had a few chances to kill the king, but each time he had the opportunity, he walked away from it.

One time King Saul was chasing David but could not find him. The king went into a cave where David happened to be hiding but Saul did not know he was there. "Now is your chance," one of David's men said. "Go on and kill

the king. God has given him into your hands." David crept forward very quietly and cut off a corner of King Saul's robe.

But David did not feel right about what he had done. "It isn't right to attack the king whom God placed in power. I should not have cut his robe." So he waited until King Saul left the cave then he went out and shouted, "My lord and king!"

King Saul turned around and David said, "Why do you listen to people who say that I wish to harm you? I could have killed you today, but I didn't. See? I cut your robe but did not hurt you."

King Saul was so surprised that he began to cry. "You are a better man than I am because you have repaid my evil with good. Now I realize that you will be a good king. Promise me that when you do become king you will not kill my family or any of my descendants!"

Another time David slipped in to King Saul's camp and found the king and his general sleeping inside a circle of other soldiers. One of David's soldiers, Abishai, crept into Saul's camp with David. They saw Saul's spear stuck in the ground next to him. "Let me take that spear and kill him right now!" Abishai begged.

"No," David said. "Don't kill him. He is the man God made king. God himself will strike him down at the right time. I will not be the one responsible for his death." So David took the spear and Saul's water jug and left the camp. He went some distance from the camp then stopped and shouted for Saul's general to wake up. "You're not protecting your king very well," David shouted. "Look, I have his spear and water jug. But notice, King Saul, that I did not harm you. Will you value my life as much as I have valued yours?" King Saul blessed David and sent him on his way.

David Is King

King Saul was the first king of Israel. God chose him to be king because the people begged for a king. Because King Saul did not honor and obey God his reign as king was about to end. The next king of Israel was David, who was just a boy when God chose him for kingship. King Saul was jealous of David because he was very popular among all the people. He tried many, many times to kill David but God always protected him.

David Becomes King *1 Samuel 31:1–6; 2 Samuel 1, 2*

The Philistines attacked King Saul's army. The Philistines were winning and as the battle raged, three of Saul's sons were killed. One of them was David's good friend, Jonathan. Then, as the battle got stronger and fiercer, the Philistines closed in on the remaining soldiers. Suddenly King Saul was badly wounded in the battle. "Take my sword and kill me,"

he begged his armor bearer. Saul didn't want the Philistines to have the privilege of killing the king of Israel. But his armor bearer was too frightened to kill the king. He wanted to honor the king's wishes, but he just could not kill his king. Saul just could not let the Philistines take his life. So he took his own sword and fell on it, killing himself. When the armor bearer saw that King Saul was dead, he took his own life too.

So Saul, three of his sons, his armor bearer, and all of his soldiers died on the same day.

A messenger arrived at David's camp and reported that King Saul and David's good friend, Jonathan, were dead. David couldn't believe it and immediately asked if the messenger was sure they were dead. The messenger reported that he saw King Saul leaning on his spear and in fact, claimed that

King Saul begged him to kill him and stop his suffering. The messenger lied that he then killed the king. David was furious that this man thought it was OK to kill the man God had chosen to be king, so he had his soldier kill the messenger.

Even though King Saul had tried many times to kill David, David was heartbroken to hear that King Saul and Jonathan were dead. He grieved for a long time for them and the loss of the entire Israelite army. When his period of mourning was over, David asked God if he should move back to Judah. God said that he should. A long time before, God had told Samuel to anoint David to be the next king of Israel after Saul. That happened when David arrived in Judah and the leaders gathered together and crowned him King of Israel.

David and Mephibosheth *2 Samuel 9*

When Jonathan and David declared their lifelong friendship for each other, Jonathan asked an important favor from David. He knew that David would one day be king and he asked that when that happened David would be kind to any of Jonathan's family who was still around. After Jonathan died, David remembered the promise but he didn't know if there were any of Saul's or Jonathan's family still alive. He called for a man named Ziba who had once been a servant of King Saul.

"Do you know if there is anyone still alive from King Saul's family?" he asked the man. "If so, I want to show God's kindness to that person."

"As a matter of fact I know that one of Jonathan's sons is still alive. His name is Mephibosheth ," Ziba said.

"Where is he?" David asked.

"He lives with another family in a town near here," Ziba said. David quickly sent a messenger to bring Mephibosheth to David. The servant brought the man to King David but Mephibosheth was terrified. He knew that his grandfather had tried many times to kill David and he was afraid that David was planning to kill him because of Saul's actions.

"Don't be afraid," David said. "I mean you no harm. I asked you to come here to see how I might help you. I promised your father a long time ago that I would always be kind to his family and I wish to honor that promise. I will give you all the land that once belonged to your grandfather, King Saul. However I would like it if you would live here in the palace with me."

Mephibosheth was overcome with thankfulness. He fell to the ground crying, "O King, why should you show such amazing kindness to me?"

David called for Ziba to come back and said to him, "I have given your master's grandson all the land that once belonged to King Saul. I would like for you and your sons and servants to farm the land for him so that there is food for his family. However Mephibosheth will stay here in the palace with me."

From that time on, Ziba and his 15 sons and 20 servants farmed the land for Mephibosheth. But Mephibosheth lived in the palace with David, as though he were one of David's sons. Ziba and his family were servants to Mephibosheth's family from that day on.

Absalom's Rebellion *2 Samuel 15, 18*

avid's son, Absalom, wanted to be king. He didn't respect his father and just wanted him to get out of the way so that he could become king. For a while they didn't even talk to each other. Finally, though, Absalom and David became friends again. But Absalom wasn't finished trying to take over the kingdom. He bought a chariot and horses and hired 50 men to

run ahead of him. He got up very early every day and went to the gate of the city. When people came to bring their problems to the king for him to settle, Absalom stopped them and asked where they were from. He sympathized with their problems and said that if he were king he would make sure to have people to hear the cases and make certain all problems got settled quickly. He said that if it were up to him, he would make sure that everyone got justice. The people were very impressed with Absalom (that was his plan) and some tried to bow before him. But he wouldn't let them. Instead he shook their hands and hugged them. Because of the way he behaved, Absalom won people's hearts and loyalty.

Absalom did this for four years, then he asked his father for permission to go to Hebron to offer a sacrifice in response to a vow he had once made. David allowed him to go but Absalom had another plan to trick his father. While he was in Hebron he went to secret messengers and spread lies to stir up a rebellion against King David. "When you hear trumpets blow you will know that I have been crowned king of Hebron."

More and more men joined Absalom and some of David's advisors hurried to Jerusalem to warn David of what Absalom was doing. David ran from Jerusalem because he knew his own son would kill him if he caught up with him. Many of his followers went with him, but Ahithophel left David and began supporting Absalom. David prayed that he would give Absalom bad advice. He sent one of his own servants, Hushai, to advise Absalom too

and asked him to try to frustrate his son's plans. David's plan worked and Absalom followed Hushai's advice. But he still searched for his father to take the kingship from him.

Things went from bad to worse and finally David divided his soldiers into three troops and placed Joab, Abishai, and Ittai to each lead a troop. They left Jerusalem to find Absalom and stop his attacks on his father. "Please though, deal gently with my son," David begged. He didn't want Absalom hurt.

When David's soldiers found Absalom the battle was strong and intense. At one point Absalom saw some of David's soldiers nearby and he hurried the donkey he was riding on to get away. Absalom had long hair and as the donkey ran beneath a tree, Absalom's hair caught in a branch and he was left hanging from the tree by his hair. One of David's soldiers saw him swinging from the tree but did not hurt him because he remembered that David wanted him to be safe. But Joab was not as kind. He stabbed Absalom with three knives until he was dead. The soldiers buried Absalom's body in a deep pit and covered it over with stones.

THE REIGN OF SOLOMON

After King David died, his son Solomon became the new king of Israel. Solomon was known for his great wisdom; in fact he was called the wisest man in the world. But even though Solomon was very wise he did some dumb things and disobeyed God. He began his reign as king by asking God to make him wise and said that he wanted wisdom more than riches. God did make him wise and also very rich. But Solomon still made some very bad choices.

Solomon Becomes King *1 Kings 1*

After King David's son Absalom died, David had more problems with another one of his sons, Adonijah, who also wanted to be king. But David had already declared that his son, Solomon, would become king after him. David was now very old and weak so Adonijah thought he could just take over the throne.

Adonijah gathered his supporters around him. He offered animal sacrifices as he planned to declare himself king. He invited some of his father's friends but did not invite Nathan (the prophet), Benaiah (who was loyal to David), or his brother, Solomon, to this sacrifice and the celebration after it. When Nathan heard that Adonijah was making sacrifices and planning to take over the throne he went to see Bathsheba, Solomon's mother. They came up with a plan to stop Adonijah. Bathsheba would go to David and tell him what Adonijah was doing. While she was with him, Nathan would come in with the same report. If David heard the news from both of them then he would believe it.

Right away Bathsheba went to David and said, "My lord, you promised me that my son, Solomon, would be king after you. So why is Adonijah now offering sacrifices and planning a banquet to celebrate becoming king?" While she was explaining this, Nathan came in and told David the same news.

When David heard Nathan's report, he said, "I promised that Solomon will be the next king and he shall be." Then he instructed his servants to put Solomon on his personal mule and take him to Gihon. When they arrived, Zadok the priest and Nathan would anoint Solomon as king.

Then when he returned to the palace Solomon would sit on David's throne. "He shall be king and may the Lord be with him," David declared.

So Zadok and Nathan, along with some other leaders, took Solomon to Gihon. He rode on David's personal mule. When they arrived they anointed him to be king. All the people there shouted, "Long live King Solomon!" and trumpets and flutes blew in celebration.

The shouting and music were so loud that Adonijah and his guests heard the noise at their own celebration banquet. *What is going on?* they wondered. Just then someone arrived announcing that Solomon was just declared king. "Solomon is already sitting on the throne!" they told the would-be king. Many royal officials ran to King David and congratulated him and wished the new king success and a long life. Meanwhile, Adonijah's guests jumped up from the banquet and ran in all directions. They were afraid for their lives since they had been part of Adonijah's attempt to steal the throne. Adonijah himself was terrified of what Solomon would do to him. He ran to the altar of God and grabbed hold of it. He begged, "Please let Solomon swear that he will not kill me!"

Solomon heard what his brother was doing and said, "If he proves to be loyal to me then he will not be harmed, but if he is not he will be killed." He called Adonijah to come before him and when his brother bowed low before him, King Solomon told him to go home. He would not be killed.

The Wisdom of Solomon *1 Kings 3*

King Solomon loved God and tried to lead the people of Israel in the way his father, David, taught him. One night he offered 1,000 burnt offerings to God. That night God spoke to Solomon in a dream and asked him, "What would you like me to give you? Ask me anything."

"O God, You were so kind and faithful to my father and You have continued Your faithfulness to me by allowing me to succeed my father as king. But I'm like a child who knows so little and now I have the responsibility of leading such a great nation. What I really need is an understanding mind. I need wisdom in leading these people so I can govern them well and quickly know right from wrong," Solomon prayed.

God was very pleased with Solomon's prayer because he asked for wisdom instead of money or power. "I will give you what you asked for," God said. "I will give you wisdom and understanding. I will also give you what you did not ask for. I will give you wealth and honor. No other king in the entire world will match you in wealth or honor. If you continue to follow and obey me I will give you a long life too."

Some time later, two women came to King Solomon and asked him to solve a problem. "Your Highness," one woman began, "this woman and I live in the same house and we each gave birth to babies—three days apart. Her baby died during the night and she got up and took my son from beside me while I was sleeping. Then she laid her dead baby boy next to me. When I woke up in the morning I thought my son was dead but then I looked closely and saw that the baby next to me wasn't mine!"

The second woman interrupted, "You're wrong! The dead baby is yours and the living baby is mine!"

"No," the first woman shouted, "the living baby is mine. You stole him!"

They argued back and forth until King Solomon stopped them. "Let me get this straight," he said. "You both claim that the living baby is yours and that the dead baby belongs to the other one. OK, we can settle this. Bring a sword to me!" he called. A servant brought a sword to the king and Solomon instructed, "Cut the living baby in half and give each mother one half of him."

The woman who was the true mother of the living baby screamed, "No! Don't hurt the baby! Let her have him but please do not hurt him."

The other woman said, "Go ahead and kill him. Then neither of us will have a living baby."

"Don't hurt the baby," King Solomon said. "Give him to the first woman. She is his true mother because she would rather give him away than have him hurt."

News of King Solomon's great wisdom quickly spread throughout the entire land. The people knew that it was a gift from God.

Solomon Builds God's Temple *1 Kings 5, 6*

God did not allow King David to build His temple because David was a soldier and fought many wars. But God did allow Solomon the privilege and responsibility of building His temple. King Solomon wrote a message to the king of Tyre and asked him to supply the lumber needed for the temple. Solomon's men would work right beside King Hiram's workers to chop down the cedar and cypress trees and cut them into logs. As payment,

Solomon promised to send 100,000 bushels of wheat and 110,000 gallons of olive oil to King Hiram. Solomon gathered 30,000 workers and divided them into three groups of 10,000 each. Each group went to work for a month at a time. Solomon also enlisted 70,000 common workers, 80,000 stonecutters, and 3,600 supervisors to work at gathering supplies for the temple.

In the fourth year of Solomon's reign as king, work on the temple began. This was 480 years after Moses led the Israelites out of slavery in Egypt. The temple was 90 feet long, 30 feet wide, and 45 feet high. A series of rooms were built around the outer walls of the temple. It was three stories high and had a winding staircase from the first floor to the second and a straight staircase up to the third floor.

Inside, the temple had wood paneled walls and ceilings. There was an inner room called the Most Holy Place at one end and the ark of the covenant was kept there. The walls and ceiling were overlaid with pure gold. In fact, he covered the inside of the entire temple with gold. Solomon placed two cherubim made of olive wood in the inner room. All the temple walls were decorated with cherubim, palm trees, and flowers and even the floors were covered with gold. The entrance to the inner room was double doors made of olive wood covered with gold and they had doorposts with five sides. The entrance to the temple itself was two folding doors of cypress wood. The doors folded back onto themselves. They had carvings of palm trees, cherubim, and open flowers and were covered with gold. The walls of the courtyard were built so that there was one layer of cedar beams on top of each three layers of cut stone.

The temple was a beautiful place that was built to honor God.

Solomon Turns from God

1 Kings 10:14-29; 11:1-13

God kept His promise to make Solomon a wealthy man. Each year Solomon received about 25 tons of gold besides what he got from taxes. He had a lot of merchant ships that brought in more wealth every three years when they came home loaded with gold, silver, ivory, apes, and peacocks. He also had 1,400 chariots and 12,000 horses.

Solomon became very famous for his great wealth and wisdom. People came from all over to hear him and to see if he was truly as wealthy as they heard.

Solomon tried to follow God most of his life but as he grew older, he made some bad choices. One of those was the choice to marry lots of wives from foreign countries. His wives worshiped false gods that they brought into Israel. Solomon began honoring the gods of his wives instead of honoring the one true God. This was the very reason God instructed His people not to marry people from other countries and faiths. Solomon ignored God's command and married 700 wives. He also had 300 mistresses.

God was not pleased that Solomon's heart turned away from Him. He was even more unhappy when Solomon built altars for his wives' false gods. God warned Solomon about his disobedience, but Solomon ignored Him. So God told him, "Since you have not kept your promise to me and have disobeyed my laws, I will take your position as king away from you. I will give it to one of your servants. However, as an honor to your father, David, I will not do this while you are still alive. I will take it away from your son. Also as an honor to your father and to my city of Jerusalem, I will allow your son to remain king of one tribe."

TROUBLE FOR ISRAEL

God told Solomon that he was going to lose his position as king of Israel because Solomon disobeyed God. Sure enough, Solomon left his kingdom and all his wealth to his son Rehoboam. But Solomon's son did not honor God. In fact, he was such a bad king that the kingdom divided. Now there was a northern kingdom and a southern kingdom.

The Kingdom Divides *1 Kings 11:26-43; 12:1-20*

Jeroboam was a son of one of Solomon's officials. Solomon had put him in charge of some work because he saw that he was very capable. One day a prophet came to him. The prophet tore his new robe into 12 pieces. "Take 10 of the pieces," he told Jeroboam. "This is what God says, 'I will give you 10 of the tribes of Israel. I will leave one tribe for Solomon's son for the sake of my servant, David.'" Solomon heard about this and tried to kill Jeroboam, but he escaped to Egypt. When Solomon died, his son Rehoboam became the king of Israel. He went to Shechem where officials had gathered to crown him king. The leaders of Israel, along with Jeroboam, went to talk to Rehoboam. "Your father put heavy taxes on us and made us work very hard. Lighten our load and we will be your loyal subjects," they said.

"Give me three days to think about it," Rehoboam answered. He went to discuss this with some of the men who had advised his father. They told him to do it because the people would then be loyal to him.

But Rehoboam rejected their advice and listened to what the younger men told him to do. "Tell the people to stop complaining or you will pile even more taxes on them and require even more labor."

Three days later the leaders and people came to hear Rehoboam's answer to their request. They were upset when Rehoboam harshly told them that he would be even tougher on them than his father had been. He rejected all their requests to make their lives easier.

"Let's go home," the people cried. "Solomon's son has no interest in helping us so we will not serve him." Rehoboam sent the leader of his labor force to restore order and subdue the people into serving him. But the people stoned the man to death. The northern tribes of Israel refused to serve Solomon's son. Instead, they made Jeroboam their king. This was exactly what God had planned. It fulfilled what God told Solomon years before.

Ravens Feed Elijah *1 Kings 16:29-34; 17:1-7*

King Ahab came to power over Israel. King Asa ruled Judah. These were the two kingdoms of divided Israel. King Ahab was more evil than any other king. He did bad things in God's sight. He even built a temple to worship the false god, Baal.

Elijah was God's servant. He told King Ahab, "The God of Israel, the God I serve, says there will be no rain or even dew on all the land until I say so."

God told Elijah to go hide at a place where the Kerith Ravine entered the Jordan River. "You can drink from the brook. I will send ravens to bring you food." Elijah would be safe there even though the land would go into a drought. No food could grow without water for the land.

Elijah did what God told him to do. He hid from King Ahab who was very angry with him. God sent ravens every morning and every night to bring him food. He drank water from the brook. Elijah stayed there until the brook dried up. No rain fell on the land the entire time he was there.

JOE MANISCALCO

The Widow's Son *1 Kings 17:8-24*

When Elijah's water supply at the Kerith Ravine dried up, God still took care of him. God told him to go to Zarephath. "There is a widow there who will give you food," God said. He had given the woman instructions.

Elijah entered the village and right away saw a woman picking up sticks. He asked her for a cup of water. When she went to get him the water, he called, "Bring me some bread too."

The woman stopped and said, "I don't have a single piece of bread in my house. I only have a little flour left and a little cooking oil. I was just picking up these sticks to cook one last loaf of bread. After that my son and I will die of starvation."

Elijah answered, "Don't be afraid. Go ahead and make your last meal but make a little loaf of bread for me first.

Afterward there will still be enough food for you and your son. God says there will always be plenty of flour and oil left in your jars until the time when God sends rain for the crops again."

The widow did what Elijah said and brought him some bread and water. After that, every time she needed to make more bread there was still flour in her jar. There was still oil in her jar. She had all she needed to feed herself and her son. No matter how much she used, there was always some left over for the next time just as God promised.

A little while later, the widow's young son became very sick. He got worse and worse and finally died. The widow was heartbroken. She sent for Elijah and said to him, "Why did you keep us alive only to let my son die now?"

"Give me your son," Elijah said. He carried the boy's body to his own room. He laid the boy's body on his bed and then prayed, "O God, why have You brought such pain on this woman who took care of me?" Elijah stretched his own body out over the boy's body. He did this three different times. Each time he prayed, "Please God, let this child's life return." God heard Elijah's prayer and gave life back to the boy. When the boy was alive again, Elijah gave him back to his mother.

The widow said, "Now I know for sure that you are a man of God and that He speaks through you."

Mt. Carmel Contest *1 Kings 18:1-40*

The drought God brought on Israel (because of King Ahab's evil ways) was in its third year. God told Elijah to go see King Ahab and tell him that rain would come soon.

Meanwhile the lack of food had become very severe. Ahab called for Obadiah, who was in charge of the palace. Obadiah followed God and had once saved 100 of the Lord's prophets from being murdered. On his way to see the king, Obadiah saw Elijah coming toward him. He fell to the ground and cried, "Is it really you?"

"Yes, it is me," Elijah answered. "Go tell your king that I am here."

"Oh, sir," Obadiah cried, "why would you want me to be killed? King Ahab has searched everywhere for you. As soon as he heard you were in one place he rushed there only to discover you were gone. I know that as soon as I tell him you are here God will sweep you up and put you down somewhere else. I have served God and even protected His prophets. Why would you want me to be killed?"

"I promise you that I will not leave," Elijah said. "I want to talk with King Ahab."

So Obadiah ran and got the king. He was not happy to see Elijah. "So you are the one who has brought all this suffering on Israel!" he said.

"I didn't bring suffering. You did, by disobeying God," Elijah responded. "You and your family have refused to worship Him. Instead you worship Baal. That is dishonoring to God. Let's put an end to this right now. Baal has 450 prophets here and Asherah has 400 prophets. I am the only prophet of God who is left. So bring all of Baal and Asherah's prophets and all the people to the top of Mt. Carmel to meet with me."

Ahab called all the prophets and all the people to the top of the mountain. Elijah was there. He said to them, "How long are you going to waver between obeying God and obeying Baal? Make up your mind—if God is God then follow Him. If Baal is God then follow him!" No one said a word. All the people just stared at Elijah.

"OK, I'm the only prophet of God left so I challenge the prophets of Baal to a contest," Elijah said. "Bring two bulls. The 450 prophets of Baal can choose whichever bull they want. Then they should cut it into pieces and put it on the altar. They must pray for Baal to send down fire to burn the sacrifice. I will do the same. The God who sends fire to burn the sacrifice is the true

God." All the people agreed to Elijah's plan.

"You go first," Elijah told the prophets of Baal. So they chose the bull they wanted. They cut it into pieces and laid it on the altar. Then they called on Baal to send down fire to burn up the offering. Nothing happened. So they danced around and shouted even louder. Still nothing happened. Elijah was watching all this and he began making fun of them.

"Maybe your god is asleep," he said. "Maybe he is out to lunch or even gone on a trip. Shout louder!" This went on all afternoon. Finally when evening came they gave up.

Now it was Elijah's turn. He called all the people around him. They crowded around as he repaired the broken altar. He picked up 12 stones, representing the 12 tribes of Israel, and used them to fix the altar. He dug a trench around the altar. He piled wood on the altar then cut up the bull and placed it on the wood. He called for men to pour four large jars of water over the whole thing. When they finished, Elijah told them to do it again and then a third time too. There was so much water that it even overflowed the trench. Elijah walked up to the altar and prayed, "O Lord, God of Abraham, Isaac, and Jacob. Prove to these people that You are God and that I am Your servant." In a grand flash of light fire shot down from the sky. It burned up the bull and all the wood. It burned up the stones and the dust. It even dried up all the water.

When the people saw the fire they shouted, "The Lord is God! The Lord is God!" The prophets of Baal and Asherah started to run away. But Elijah ordered the people to capture them. He took all of them down to the valley and killed them.

The Chariot of Fire *2 Kings 2:1-18*

E lijah continued to obey God and serve Him. God was so pleased with Elijah that He planned to take him to Heaven without having to die first. Another man traveled with Elijah.

His name was Elisha and he was learning how to serve God. One day Elijah said to Elisha, "God has called me to go to Bethel. You stay here."

"No. I will not be separated from

you," Elisha said. "I want to go with you." So they went on together.

When they arrived in Bethel some prophets came to Elisha and said, "Did you know that God is going to take your master, Elijah, away from you today?"

"Yes, I know!" Elisha shouted. "But I don't want to talk about it."

"God has told me to go to Jericho," Elijah told Elisha. "You stay here."

"No, I will not be separated from you," Elisha said. "Please let me go with you." So they went on together.

When they arrived, a group of prophets from Jericho said to Elisha, "Did you know that God is going to take your master away from you today?"

"Yes, I know," he answered.

Then Elijah said, "Stay here, Elisha, for the Lord has told me to go to the Jordan River."

But once again, Elisha said, "No, I want to go with you." So they went on together.

Fifty prophets also went with them. They watched as Elijah took off his robe and slapped it on the waters of the Jordan River. They saw the river water divide and the two men walk through on dry ground.

When they got to the other side, Elijah asked, "What can I do for you, Elisha, before I am taken away?"

"Please, allow me to become your successor," Elisha answered.

"That's a hard thing for me to grant," Elijah said. "But if you see me when I am taken away then your request will be granted. If you don't see me then it will not be granted."

Suddenly a chariot of fire swooped down. It was pulled by horses of fire. It came right between the two men. Elijah was carried away by a whirlwind. He was taken to Heaven.

Elisha saw the whole thing happen!

Elisha picked up Elijah's robe and returned to the Jordan River. He struck the water with it as Elijah had done. The water parted and Elisha walked through on dry ground. When the group of prophets saw this whole thing they shouted, "Elisha is Elijah's successor!" They ran to meet him and offered to send a search party for Elijah. "Maybe he was dropped down on a mountain top or in a valley," they said. Elisha told them not to search for Elijah but they insisted. So he let them look for Elijah. Fifty men searched for three days but they did not find him.

When they returned to tell Elisha that they couldn't find him, he said, "I told you so."

STORIES OF ELISHA

Elisha saw his friend and mentor, Elijah, taken to Heaven in a chariot of fire. God loved Elijah so much that he didn't even have to die to get to Heaven! Elisha wanted more than anything to take over God's work and sure enough, that's just what God wanted too. Elisha saw his friend taken up to Heaven and that meant that God's work was left for Elisha to do. God gave him wisdom and strength.

Elisha Solves a Problem *2 Kings 2:19-22*

Elisha had picked up Elijah's coat when that great prophet was taken to Heaven in a chariot of fire. Now Elisha was carrying on God's work with God's wisdom and power guiding him.

One day the leaders of the town of Jericho came to Elisha with a serious problem.

"Sir, you can see that this town is in a beautiful place but it is difficult to live here because the water is bad. The land is bad too. It doesn't grow healthy crops. So we try to live here but the water is not drinkable and the land doesn't grow food for the people."

Elisha told the leaders to bring him a brand new bowl that was filled with salt. When they brought it, Elisha took it out to the spring that supplied water for the city and he threw the salt into it. "This is what the Lord says," Elisha announced. "I have made this water good so it will no longer cause illness or death." Sure enough the water was good for the people to drink again and it supplied the land with nourishment to grow food!

A Room for Elisha *2 Kings 4:8-17*

Elisha traveled around from town to town solving problems for people and encouraging them to obey and follow God. One day he visited the town of Shunem. A rich woman saw him in the town and invited him to come home with her for dinner. After that day, any time Elisha came to Shunem he would have dinner with this woman and her husband. But just serving dinner

to God's prophet wasn't good enough for the rich woman. She had another idea. "Why don't we build a room for Elisha?" she asked her husband. "We can make a room for him up on the roof of our house and put a bed, a table, a chair, and a lamp in it. That way when this man of God passes through Shunem he will always know that he has a place to stay." So that's what they did.

Elisha was pleased to have a place to stay and he used it often. One time when he was resting in his room he had a thought. He called his servant, Gehazi, to go get the generous woman. When she came to the door, Elisha asked, "What can I do to repay your kindness? Would you like me to put in a good word for you with the king or the commander of the army?"

"That won't be necessary," the woman said. "My family takes good care of me. I don't really need anything."

But Elisha couldn't get rid of the thought that he should do something kind for her. He asked Gehazi for ideas and his servant had one. "The woman's husband is pretty old and she doesn't have any children to take care of her," Gehazi said. "Maybe she would like to have a son."

Elisha thought that was a wonderful idea so he told the woman that by that time next year she would have her very own son. At first the woman was afraid to believe Elisha. Once she saw that he was serious she was overjoyed. She couldn't believe that his news was true. But sure enough, about a year later the woman had a baby boy.

The Generous Woman's Son *2 Kings 4:18-37*

The rich lady of Shunem was thrilled to have a son. She was grateful to Elisha for him because she knew that Elisha had prayed for God to give her a child.

One day the little boy went out to the fields where his father was working. He liked to visit his father there. While he was there he began complaining that he had a terrible headache. "My head hurts! It hurts so much!" he cried. His father had one of the servants carry the boy back to the house and get his mother to care for him. The servant carried the boy home and the rich woman of Shunem sat with her son on her lap all morning. About noontime

the little boy died. The heartbroken mother carried his body up to the rooftop, to the room she had made for Elisha. She carefully laid her son's body on Elisha's bed and left him there. Then she sent an urgent message to her husband, "Send a donkey and a servant here quickly. I must go see the man of God right away."

Her husband didn't know why she needed to go so quickly. He knew it wasn't a religious holiday but he didn't argue with his wife. He sent the donkey and the servant. The woman got on the donkey and told the servant to hurry to where Elisha was.

When she got close to where Elisha was he saw her and recognized her right away. Elisha sent his servant to meet her. "Is everything alright with you?" Gehazi asked. "Is your husband alright and your son?"

"Yes," the woman told Gehazi, "everything is fine."

But when she got to Elisha she fell to the ground crying, and grabbed hold of his feet. Gehazi tried to push her away from his master but the woman would not let go. Finally Elisha said, "No, Gehazi. Leave her alone. Something terrible is wrong but the Lord has not yet told me what it is."

Finally the woman was able to stop crying enough to speak. "It was you who told me that I would have a son," she said. "You knew that I thought it was too good to be true."

Immediately Elisha told Gehazi to get ready to travel. "Don't talk to anyone," he said. "Just go quickly to the boy and lay my staff on his face." Gehazi obeyed.

But the sad mother said, "I'm not going anywhere unless you go home with me. I mean it." Elisha didn't argue with the woman but returned to her house with her right away.

Elisha went into the room where the boy's body was lying. He shut the door behind him and prayed to God. Then he lay down on top of the boy's body. As he laid there the boy's body began to grow warm again. Life was returning! Elisha got up and walked around the room a few times, and then he lay down on top of the boy again. This time the boy sneezed seven times and opened his eyes! "Call the boy's mother," Elisha instructed Gehazi. When she came in he said, "Here is your son." The woman was filled with joy! She picked up her son and took him downstairs.

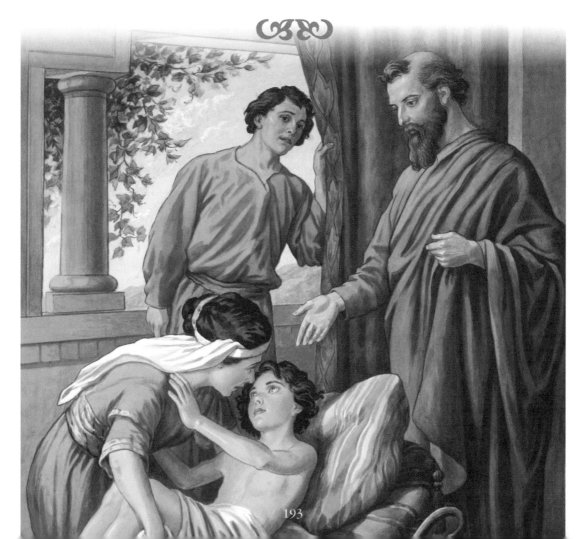

Naaman Is Cured   *2 Kings 5:1-19*

Naaman was the commander of the army of the king of Aram. The king was fond of Naaman because God had given them many great victories. But even though he was a good military commander, Naaman was stricken with the skin disease called leprosy. It was a terrible disease that ate away the skin. It was very also contagious so people who had leprosy had to live away from other people. They couldn't live with their families because they might give the disease to them.

There was a servant girl in Naaman's house. She was actually a slave who had been captured when the army invaded Israel. She lived with Naaman's family and served his wife. One day the little girl told her mistress that Naaman should go to see the prophet in Samaria. "I know he can heal the master's leprosy," the girl said. Naaman told the king of Aram what the girl said and the king encouraged him to go visit the prophet. The king of Aram even gave Naaman a letter of introduction to give to the king of Israel. Naaman loaded up 750 pounds of silver, 150 pounds of gold, and 10 sets of clothing as gifts to give the king. The letter of introduction said who Naaman was and asked that he be healed of leprosy.

The king of Israel read the letter and was quite upset. "What am I supposed to do? Heal a man who has leprosy? I can't do that. I fear that the king of Aram is just trying to find a reason to invade our land!"

Elisha heard about the letter and how upset the king was. He sent a messenger to ask, "Why are you so upset? Send Naaman to me and he will learn that there is a true prophet here in Israel."

Naaman went to Elisha's house and waited at the door but Elisha didn't come out. Instead he sent a messenger who said, "Go wash yourself seven times in the Jordan River. Then your skin will be healed and the leprosy will be gone."

Naaman got angry that Elisha didn't come himself to heal him. "I thought that surely the prophet would come himself to heal my disease," he said. "Why should I wash in the Jordan River? We have better rivers back home." Naaman left in a storm of anger.

But his own officers tried to convince him to listen to the messenger. "Sir, if the prophet had told you to do something really difficult in order to be healed, you would do it. Why not do this simple thing and see what happens?" they asked. They convinced Naaman to give it a try so he went down to the

Jordan River and dipped his body in it seven times as he was instructed. After the seventh time, his body was healed—the leprosy was gone!

So Naaman went back to Elisha's house and Naaman stood before him and said, "I know now that there is no greater God in all the world than the God of Israel. Please accept these gifts I've brought to you."

Elisha refused the gifts. Then Naaman asked permission to take two donkey loads of soil with him from Elisha's home and he promised that he would never offer sacrifices to any other god except the God of Israel again.

Eyes to See *2 Kings 6:8-23*

When the army of Aram was fighting against the army of Israel, the king of Aram would make battle plans of places to attack the Israelites. But God always had Elisha warn the king of Israel not to go to those places. The king of Aram got very upset because he thought one of his officers must be a traitor. He insisted that the traitor come forward

and confess but the officers all denied that they gave information to the Israelites. "It's Elisha, the prophet," the officers said. "He knows everything you say, even the things you say in private." The king ordered his soldiers to find Elisha so he could send soldiers to capture him.

The report came back that Elisha was at Dothan. So the king sent his army with many chariots to surround that city. Early the next morning, Elisha's servant got up and he saw soldiers and horses and chariots everywhere he looked. He ran to Elisha and told him about the armies. "What do we do?" he cried. The servant was terrified.

"Don't worry," Elisha said. "There are a lot more soldiers on our side than on theirs." The servant didn't know what Elisha was talking about though because they didn't have any soldiers. "O Lord," Elisha prayed, "open my servant's eyes. Let him see!" God answered that prayer and when the servant looked around he saw that the hillside was filled with horses and chariots of fire—God's army!

When the army of Aram started down the hillside toward Elisha, the prophet prayed again "O Lord, please make the soldiers of Aram blind." God did what Elisha asked. When the soldiers were blinded, Elisha went to them and shouted, "The man you are looking for is over that way. Follow me and I'll take you to him." The soldiers followed him and he led them to Samaria. Then Elisha prayed that their sight would be restored.

Once they could see again the soldiers discovered they were in Samaria. The king of Israel shouted to Elisha, "Should we kill them?"

"No," Elisha answered. "We don't kill prisoners of war, do we? Give them food and drink and send them on their way." So the king made a great banquet for them and then sent them back to their own land.

JUDAH'S LAST DAYS

Judah just couldn't seem to get it right. God sent them warning after warning through His prophets. The prophets warned the nation that they needed to obey God. They urged Judah to repent of their sins and straighten up their lives. But the people just ignored God and the prophets and kept right on doing what they wanted to do. They should have known from past history that God wouldn't put up with their disrespect and disobedience. The nation of Judah was about to come crashing down.

Isaiah's Vision *Isaiah 6:1-13*

The prophet Isaiah had a vision. He saw something that ended up being a message from God for him. In this vision Isaiah saw God sitting on a throne and the robe He was wearing was so long that it filled the entire temple. There were six-winged seraphims flying around the throne. With two of their wings they covered their eyes. With two they covered their feet and they flew with the other two. In loud voices they all sang, "Holy, holy, holy is the Lord Almighty! The whole earth is filled with His glory!" The singing was so loud that it shook the building to its very foundation. The whole room filled with smoke.

Isaiah thought he was done for. "My destruction is sealed! I know I'm a sinful man and that the whole human race is sinful. However, I've seen the Lord himself!"

Isaiah saw one of the seraphim fly to the altar and pick up a burning coal with a pair of tongs. The seraphim touched Isaiah's lips with the burning coal and said, "See, this coal has touched your lips. Now your sin is forgiven."

Then Isaiah heard the Lord asking a question, "Whom should I send to bring a message to my people?"

Isaiah said, "I will go. Send me!"

God said, "Yes, I want you to go. Tell my people that they may hear my words but they won't understand my message. You will see my work, but you won't understand it. I will harden their hearts and close their ears and their eyes."

"How long must I do this work for You?" Isaiah asked.

God replied, "You must do this until their cities are destroyed and no one is left in them; until their houses are empty and the whole country is a disaster. Do not stop warning them until everyone has been sent away. Even if only a tenth of the people are still here I will make sure the land is invaded again. Israel will be like a stump or a tree that is cut down. However, the stump will grow again from a holy seed."

Josiah's Great Find *2 Kings 22:1–23:30*

Josiah was eight years old when he became king of Judah and he reigned for 31 years. Josiah obeyed God and the Lord was happy with him. He followed the example of King David before him.

When he had been king for 18 years, he sent Shaphan to see Hilkiah the high priest. He wanted to have him count the money that had been collected to repair the temple. It would be used to pay the workers. Josiah knew that the supervisors there were honest so he wasn't worried about that.

When Shaphan arrived Hilkiah told him that he had made an interesting discovery. "I have found the book of the Law in the Lord's temple!" he said.

He gave the scroll to Shaphan and he read it.

Shaphan returned to King Josiah and reported that the money had been given to the temple workers. Then Shaphan told him that the priest had given him a scroll and he read it to the king. When Josiah heard what was in the scroll he was very upset. Then he gave these orders to Hilkiah, "Go to the temple and speak to the Lord for me and for all the people of Judah. Ask about what is written in this book of the Law. The Lord's anger is burning

against us because we haven't obeyed what this scroll says."

So Hilkiah consulted with a prophetess named Huldah. She told him that the Lord declared, "I will destroy this city because the people have abandoned me and worshiped false gods. I am angry with them for everything they have done. Go to the king and tell him that I will delay my punishment because I know his heart was saddened by what he read in the book of the Law."

King Josiah called together all the leaders of Judah and he read to them the entire book of the Covenant that had been discovered in the temple. He pledged to lead the people and the nation in obeying the Law. He tore down all the temples to false gods. He removed all evidences that Judah had been worshiping idols. He brought priests back to Jerusalem who had been living in other towns. Josiah led the people in returning to the worship and obedience of God.

Hezekiah's Illness *Isaiah 38:1-22*

King Hezekiah of Judah became very ill and the prophet Isaiah went to visit him. Isaiah said, "The Lord says, 'Get your life in order because you will die from this illness.'"

When Hezekiah heard this he prayed to God, "Remember O Lord, that I have tried to be faithful to You. I have tried to obey You and do what is pleasing in Your sight." Then the king cried.

The Lord gave Isaiah a message, "Go back to the king and tell him, 'This is what the Lord, the God of David says: 'I have heard your prayer and seen your tears. I will add 15 years to your life and I will rescue you and this city from the king of Assyria. This is the sign that the Lord will give you to prove that He will do what He promises. He will cause the sun's shadow to move 10 steps backward on the sundial of Ahaz!'" Sure enough the shadow moved backward 10 steps!

DANIEL AND HIS FRIENDS

Once again God's people were taken captive by another nation. This happened often to God's people and sometimes it was because of their disobedience to Him. This time the nation of Babylon captured them. The most interesting stories of this time period center around a man named Daniel. He was just a boy when he became a servant in the Babylonian king's court. But even as a boy, Daniel had a strong faith in God and he tried to obey God all his life.

Special Training *Daniel 1*

S ome of the boys captured by the Babylonians were put into a special training program. The king of Babylon ordered that the strongest, healthiest, and best-looking young men be put in this program. He wanted

the smartest boys from royal families who had been given good educations. He wanted young men who would have good sense about how to serve and behave in the palace. The king ordered that the boys should be taught the language and the literature of their new country. They were to be given the best food from the king's own kitchen. The training period was three years long and then some of the boys would become part of the king's staff of advisers in the royal court.

Daniel and three of his friends were chosen for this training program. Being chosen for the program was an honor and it meant they had good food to eat and didn't have to do a lot of hard physical work. But Daniel had a problem with it. Daniel felt that eating the special food given to them would make him unclean before God and he didn't want to sin in that way. So Daniel asked the official in charge of him and his friends for other food. This man had great respect for Daniel so he didn't get angry with him. But he was frightened. "The king has ordered that you eat this food," he said. "If you become weak and skinnier than the other boys, the king may have me killed for not doing my duty."

But Daniel had a plan. "Let my friends and me eat only vegetables and water for 10 days," he said. "At the end of that test see how we look compared to the boys who are still eating the king's food. After that you can decide whether or not to let us continue with our

special diet. We will do whatever you say." The official agreed to this plan. So for 10 days Daniel and his three friends ate vegetables and drank water while the rest of the boys ate the king's food and had his finest wines.

At the end of the 10 day test period, Daniel and his friends were stronger and healthier than any of the other boys. The official was glad to let them continue their special diet. God also blessed these four boys with special understanding for all the things they were being taught. They learned more easily than any of the other boys. God gave Daniel special understanding and abilities to interpret the meaning of dreams.

When the three year training period was over, all the boys in the program were taken to the king. He interviewed each one of them and was most impressed by Daniel and his three friends. He chose them to be a part of his staff of advisers and found their advice to be 10 times better than that of any of his other staff people.

Four Men in a Fire *Daniel 3*

King Nebuchadnezzar of Babylon wanted the people of his land to worship him. He ordered a giant golden statue to be made of himself. It was 90 feet tall and nine feet wide. The king ordered that when people heard music played they should bow down to his statue. The punishment for refusing to bow to it was to be thrown into a blazing hot furnace. So whenever the people heard music from a flute, horn, or other instrument they

immediately bowed before the king's statue and worshiped the king. But not every person in the land obeyed this new law. Three men refused to bow to the king's statue. Some of the king's advisers went to the king and pointed out that Shadrach, Meshach, and Abednego were disobeying the command to bow down to the statue. "Sir, you said that the punishment is to be thrown into a fiery furnace. You must punish these men," they said.

The king was very angry when he heard that the three men refused to bow to his statue. They were brought before him and he said, "I will give you one more chance to obey me. If you bow down and worship the statue when you hear the music then all will be well. But if you refuse, you will be thrown into the blazing hot furnace."

"Sir, if we are thrown into the furnace we know that our God is able to save us. He will rescue us from your power, your majesty. But even if He doesn't, we will never bow down to your statue or worship your gods," the three men said.

Nebuchadnezzaar was so angry he ordered that the furnace be made seven times hotter than it usually was. Then he ordered some of the strongest men in his army to tie up the three boys and throw them into the furnace. The fire was so hot that the soldiers were killed by the flames when they got close to it. Shadrach, Meshach, and Abednego were securely tied up and they fell down in the middle of the flames. Suddenly he jumped to his feet and shouted, "How many men did we throw into the furnace?"

"Three, Sir," was the answer.

"Weren't they tied up?" the king asked.

"Yes, Sir. Tied up tightly," a soldier answered.

"Then why do I see four men walking around in the flames? They aren't tied up. They aren't hurt by the flames at all. The fourth man looks like a god or an angel," the king said. He went to the door of the furnace and called for Shadrach, Meshach, and Abednego to come out.

When they came out, all the king's officials went to look at them. They were amazed that the boys were not burned at all; in fact, they didn't even smell like smoke!

The king was so impressed that he declared, "Praise to the God of Shadrach, Meshach, and Abednego! His angel rescued these servants because they trusted Him. They disobeyed my command in order to obey their God and He protected them. Because of that, I decree that no one should speak a word against their God. No other God rescues like their God!"

The Handwriting on the Wall *Daniel 5*

Several years after the fiery furnace incident, a new king ruled Babylon. King Belshazzar gave a great feast for all of his royal friends. Thousands of people sat around drinking wine and eating rich food. While his guests were enjoying themselves, the king ordered his servants to bring in the gold and silver cups that the previous king had taken from the temple in Jerusalem. He poured wine into them and let his guests drink from them. They drank toasts to their false gods.

At the very moment they were making their toasts they saw the fingers of a man's hand writing on the wall of the king's palace. When the king saw the hand his face turned pale because

he was terrified. He was so scared that his knees shook and he had to lean on something because he couldn't stand up.

The king called for all of his wise men to come and read the handwriting on the wall. He wanted to know what it said. But none of them could tell him. The king promised great wealth and honor to the man who could explain it. But still, no one could understand it. That made the king even more afraid. Since the king was frightened, all of his servants and even his officials were frightened too. The king's mother heard what was going on and she told her son, "Don't be afraid. There is a man right here in your kingdom who has the help of his God to understand things like this. During the reign of King Nebuchadnezzar this man was found to have great wisdom and understanding. Call for the man named Daniel and he will explain the handwriting."

King Belshazzar immediately sent for Daniel and asked him if he could explain the handwriting. "My wisest advisers cannot read this but I have been told that you will be able to read it and explain it," the king said. The king offered to give Daniel honor, fame, and power in the kingdom if he would explain the handwriting.

"Keep your gifts," Daniel said. "I will explain the handwriting but I do not want your gifts. The king before you gave great honor to God and because of that God made him so great that people from many nations feared him. But when his heart was hardened toward God, he was brought down. You are his successor and you knew all this happened, yet you have chosen to be proud and defy God. Since you have not yielded to God you will be destroyed too. The handwriting says that God has numbered your days. It means you have been weighed on the scales and failed the test. Lastly, it means that your kingdom will be divided and given to the Medes and the Persians."

That very night Belshazzar was murdered and Darius the Mede took control of the kingdom.

Daniel in the Lions' Den *Daniel 6*

Darius the Mede divided the kingdom into 120 provinces and appointed a prince to manage each one. Then he chose Daniel and two others to be administrators over the provinces. Because of his great wisdom, Darius planned to place Daniel in charge of all the other administrators.

They were not happy about that. But Daniel's faithfuness and honesty had won over King Darius so they knew they had to find some way to make the king angry at him. They definitely did not want to be subject to Daniel.

The other men came up with a plan. They went to King Darius and suggested

that he should make a law that for the next 30 days no one could pray to any god or human except the king himself. They also suggested that anyone who broke that law should be thrown into a den of lions. The king accepted their praise and liked the suggestion that he should make this law. So he signed the law and sealed it with his own seal.

Daniel heard about the law but he went home and knelt down next to the window and prayed, just as he did three times every day. Nothing would stop him from praying to God. The officials who wanted to get Daniel in trouble were spying on him and saw him kneeling next to the window. They immediately went to the king and said, "Sir, remember the law you signed that the people can pray to no one except you? Well, it has been broken by your servant, Daniel. We saw him praying to his God. He must be thrown into the lions' den because that's what the law states."

King Darius knew right away that he had been tricked by men who were jealous of Daniel but he couldn't do any-

thing about it. He tried to find some way around it but there simply wasn't any. The law was signed and it had to be enforced. Finally, he ordered that Daniel be brought to him. "May the God you serve so faithfully protect you," the king said. Then Daniel was thrown into a pit full of hungry lions and a stone was pushed across the opening so he couldn't escape and so no one could rescue him. The king put his royal seal on the stone. Then the king went back to his palace and spent the night fasting because he was so concerned about Daniel.

Early the next morning the king rushed to the lions' den and called out, "Daniel, did your God save you?"

Daniel answered, "Long live the king! My God did save me. He sent his angel to keep the mouths of the lions closed so they would not hurt me. I have done nothing wrong to you, O king."

The king was very happy and ordered that Daniel be lifted out of the pit. Then he called for the men who had tricked him to be thrown into the pit themselves!

THE STORY OF QUEEN ESTHER

There comes a time in each person's life when he or she has to make a choice about how to live life. For a young Jewish girl that day certainly came. Esther was an orphan who lived with a dear relative. Mordecai taught her to honor and obey God with her life. But when this little Jewish girl—a girl with no parents, from a people without a country of their own—was chosen to be queen of the land where her nation of people were living, she had some tough choices to make.

A New Queen Is Chosen *Esther 1, 2*

The king of Persia threw a party—a big party that lasted for six months! All the important people in his kingdom were invited. That party ended and then the king held a special banquet for all the palace servants and officials. That banquet lasted for seven days. It was held in the courtyard of the palace which was beautifully decorated with white and blue banners with purple ribbons. There were gold and silver couches on the marble floor. Drinks were served in gold cups and everyone could have as much as they wanted. The queen of Persia gave a banquet for the women of the palace at the same time as the king's banquet.

On the seventh day of the king's banquet, the king commanded that Queen Vashti be brought into his banquet. He wanted her to wear her royal crown and let all the men see her great beauty. But when that command was given to Queen Vashti, she refused to come! That made the king very angry with her. He consulted his advisers

about what to do. They told him that he couldn't let Vashti get away with refusing him because then all the other women in the kingdom would think they could stand up to their husbands too. Their suggestion was that Queen Vashti be forever banished from the king's presence. Once that news got out all the husbands of the kingdom would receive proper respect from their wives. The king liked the idea so he banished Vashti and let the whole kingdom know about it.

But once his anger cooled down the king realized what he had done. He knew he needed a new queen. So the king appointed agents throughout the land to find the most beautiful women in their region and bring them to the palace. These women would be given beauty treatments and then the one the king chose would become his new queen.

There was a Jewish man right there in the same city as the palace who was named Mordecai. His young cousin, Esther, lived with him. When her parents died he adopted her and raised her as his own daughter. Esther was very beautiful so she was chosen to be one of the young girls in the program to become queen. The man in charge of all the women was very impressed with Esther. He gave her special treatment and a special diet. He also assigned servants to her. Esther did not tell anyone in the palace that she was a Jew. Mordecai told her not to mention it.

Esther had a full year of beauty treatments before she was taken to meet the king. When she met the king he was amazed at her beauty and he loved her right away. He put the crown on her head and declared her queen. Queen Esther's cousin, Mordecai, became a palace official.

A Special Request *Esther 3–6*

Everyone loved beautiful Queen Esther and things were going quite well until a man named Haman got upset. Haman was the most powerful man in the kingdom except for the king himself. He liked being powerful and he wanted everyone's respect. Haman made a decree that all the other officials in the kingdom should bow to him whenever he passed by. Everyone did, except Queen Esther's cousin, Mordecai. He refused to bow even when other officials challenged him about it. Those officials went to Haman and asked what should be done about Mordecai's refusal. Haman knew that Mordecai was a Jew so his plan for getting back at Mordecai was to destroy all the Jews in the

entire land. He convinced the king that it was a good idea to wipe all the Jews out of Persia because their beliefs and loyalties were so different from those of all the other people. The king agreed to let Haman kill the Jews but he did not know that Mordecai and Queen Esther were related or that the queen was a Jew. When Mordecai heard what Haman's plans were, he went to Queen Esther to ask for her help in saving their people. "Maybe you were made queen for such a time as this," he said to her.

Esther came up with a plan and the first step was to invite King Xerxes and Haman to a dinner. Haman was honored to be invited to the queen's dinner and even more pleased when she invited him to another dinner the next night. That made him feel important. But when he left the first dinner he passed by Mordecai, who still refused to bow to him. He was angrier than ever. Haman's wife and friends suggested that he have a gallows built and hang Mordecai on it before the second dinner. Then he could enjoy the dinner because he would know that Mordecai was dead. Haman liked that idea and ordered the gallows built.

That night the king couldn't sleep so he requested that the book of historical records of his kingdom be read to him. In the records was a story of how one man had saved the king from a plot to kill him. That brave man was Mordecai! Right at the time the king made this discovery Haman came to ask the king's permission to hang Mordecai on the gallows. But before he could ask his question the king asked Haman, "What honor should be given to a man who truly pleases me?" Well, Haman thought the king was talking about him. So Haman suggested that the honored man should wear the king's robe and ride on the king's horse through the town. "Great idea," the king said. "I will do that for Mordecai. Make sure that happens for me, Haman!" Haman did everything the king said to do for Mordecai, but he wasn't happy about it.

The next night at Queen Esther's dinner, the king asked, "My queen, what can I do for you? I will do anything; even give you up to half of my kingdom!"

Queen Esther answered, "If you really want to please me, save my life and the lives of my people! For a decree has come from your palace to have us all killed!"

"Who would dare to make such a decree?" the king asked.

"Haman!" the queen answered. The king was so angry that he decided to have Haman hung on the very gallows where Haman had intended to kill Mordecai! Queen Esther saved Mordecai and all the Jewish people!

God's People Return

God's people were captives in foreign lands for many, many years. Eventually God allowed them to return to Judah. That happened in three stages over several years. The first step was under Zerubbabel, the second under Ezra, and the third under Nehemiah. Imagine the joy of the Jewish people at returning home and no longer being captives or slaves but having freedom in their own land!

The Long Trek Home *Ezra 1, 2*

The Jewish people had been homeless for decades! They were captives (slaves) in Babylon and then Persia conquered Babylon so they were slaves to them. Finally, in the first year of King Cyrus's reign in Persia, God softened his heart toward the Jews. The king wrote a proclamation that said, "The God of Heaven has given me all the kingdoms of Earth.

He has appointed me to build Him a temple in Jerusalem in the land of Judah. Therefore, all of God's people may return to Jerusalem. People who live near any Jews should contribute silver and gold and supplies for their journey to Jerusalem. Give them livestock and an offering to help build the temple."

About the same time, God moved in the hearts of the leaders of the Jewish people. He gave them a desire to return to Jerusalem to start the work of rebuilding the temple. The people who lived near the Jews gave them silver and gold and animals and all kinds of offerings for the journey and for the supplies for the temple to be built.

King Cyrus himself brought out the things that King Nebuchadnezzar had taken from the temple when he captured the Jews. Those items had been put in the temples to his own gods. About 5,400 gold and silver items were returned to the Jews.

A total of 42,360 people returned to Judah plus almost 8,000 servants. They took over 8,000 donkeys, mules, horses, and camels with them. They were a very large group of people and animals.

Rebuilding the Walls *Nehemiah 1–6*

Nehemiah served in the court of King Artaxerxes of Persia. One day the king noticed that Nehemiah was very sad. "What are you sad about?" he asked. Nehemiah told him that he was sad because the city of Jerusalem, God's city, was in ruins and the gates had been burned down. "How can I help?" the king asked.

Nehemiah said a quick prayer before answering, "Please allow me travel there and rebuild the walls of that great

city. Grant me wood from your forests to do that and to repair the temple gates and to build a home for myself." The king granted Nehemiah's request.

When he arrived in Jerusalem, Nehemiah went around the city at night-time and inspected the walls. He was embarrassed at the disgrace into which the city had fallen. He told the city officials about his plan to rebuild the wall and they enthusiastically supported him. Many people of the various tribes came to help but there were some who opposed the building. Some Samaritans made fun of the Jews for even thinking they could rebuild the wall. "Look, they are pulling burned stones out of the rubble and reusing them! If something as small as a fox walks on that wall it will collapse again!" they said. Nehemiah prayed for God to show them they were wrong and to protect the workers.

When the wall was rebuilt to half of its normal height the people were tired. There was a lot of rubble to be moved before they could even work on the wall itself. It was hard work. Meanwhile their enemies were already planning to attack and knock the wall down again. Nehemiah set up guards around the city and made sure that the enemies knew they

had heard of their plans. From then on half of the men worked on the wall and half stood guard. A trumpeter stayed with Nehemiah so he could blow a warning to all the men if the city was attacked. Nehemiah, his servants, guards, and family never took off their clothes and never went anywhere without their weapons; even to get a drink of water.

Fifty-two days after the work on the wall began, it was finished. When the enemies of the Jews heard that, they were frightened. They knew that God was with His people, helping them and protecting them.

THE STORY OF JONAH

Jonah ran away from God. He didn't want to obey God because he wanted to do things his own way. Of course, it is not possible to hide from God. He knew where Jonah was. God gave Jonah time to think about his disobedience and then gave him a second chance to obey. Jonah became the first foreign missionary—a man God sent to another country to teach people about Him.

Running Away from God *Jonah 1, 2*

God had a special job for Jonah. "Go to Nineveh and tell the people that they must stop being so wicked. They must begin obeying me." Jonah didn't want to go to Nineveh so he went in the opposite direction. He got on a ship that was sailing for Tarshish. Jonah thought he could run from God.

But when the ship got out on the open sea God sent a powerful storm. It was so bad that the sailors on the ship were afraid they were going to die. They shouted for their gods to save them. They threw cargo over the sides of the ship. But nothing made the storm stop. The whole time Jonah was below deck, sound asleep. The captain came down and said, "How can you sleep? Get up and pray to your God. Maybe he will have mercy on us and spare our lives!"

The crew tried to figure out which one of them had made their gods angry enough to cause the terrible storm. Jonah's name kept coming up. "What have you done to cause this powerful storm?" they asked him.

Jonah answered, "I am a Hebrew and I worship the Lord, the God of Heaven. I am running away from Him."

The sailors were terrified! "Why did

you do this to us? The storm is getting worse all the time. What are we going to do?" they cried.

"Throw me into the sea," Jonah told them. "If you do, the storm will stop because it's all my fault." The sailors didn't want to but the storm kept getting worse and worse. Finally they had no choice but to throw Jonah overboard. When they did the storm stopped immediately.

God arranged for a great big fish to come along right then and swallow Jonah. He was inside the fish for three days and three nights. Jonah prayed to God from inside the fish and asked for forgiveness for his disobedience and for another chance to obey God. After he prayed, God ordered the big fish to spit up Jonah onto the shore—and it did.

Preaching in Nineveh *Jonah 3, 4*

As soon as the big fish spit out Jonah, God once again told him to go to Nineveh to deliver His message. Jonah obeyed this time and ran straight to Nineveh. The city was so big that it took three days just to see all of it. As Jonah entered the city he shouted, "Forty days from now Nineveh will be destroyed!" The people listened to him and believed his message. From the most important person to the poorest person, he fasted and wore sackcloth to show his sorrow. Even the king stepped down from his throne and took off his royal robe to wear sackcloth. He sent a decree

throughout the city. "No one, not even the animals, may eat or drink anything. Everyone must wear sackcloth and pray earnestly to God. Everyone must turn from their evil ways and stop all the violence. Maybe God will have pity on us and not destroy us."

When God saw that the people were stopping their wicked ways and turning to Him, He had mercy on them and didn't destroy them. That made Jonah angry . . . really angry! "I knew You would do something like that!" he shouted. "That's why I ran away in the first place. I knew that You are so loving and compassionate that You would forgive them. Just kill me. Let me die. I'd rather be dead than alive right now."

"What are you so angry about?" God asked.

Jonah went outside the city and built a shelter to sit under where he could sit and wait to see what happened to the city. God made a plant with big leaves grow and spread its leaves over Jonah, shading him from the sun. Jonah was very grateful for the plant. But God then made a worm that ate through the stem of the big plant so that it died. The sun grew hot and Jonah did not have the shade of the plant leaves. He got so hot that he prayed that God would just let him die.

God said, "Is it right for you to be angry because the plant died?"

"Yes," Jonah shouted, "angry enough to die!"

God said, "You feel sorry about the plant even though you did nothing to make it grow. Plants have short lives anyway. But the city of Nineveh has over 120,000 people living there who do not know about me. Shouldn't I feel sorry for them?"

The New Testament

He Came Before

From the first time Adam and Eve tasted the forbidden fruit, God had a plan for bridging the gap their sin caused. He can not be in the presence of evil, selfishness, or sin of any kind. That means that no one would ever be able to join Him in His Heaven. God made a plan to change that. He sent His only Son, Jesus, to Earth. Jesus lived as a human being and taught people how to live for God. Before Jesus was born, though, there was another baby born who had an important job to do.

Zechariah and the Angel *Luke 1:5-25*

Zechariah was a Jewish priest. He and his wife, Elizabeth, had no children even though they wanted to be parents. They were both very old so they didn't think they would ever have children.

One day Zechariah was serving in the temple and was chosen to be the one priest to go into the inner room of the temple and burn incense to God. While he was in the inner room there was a big crowd of people outside praying. It was an honor to be the priest chosen to do this.

While Zechariah was alone in the inner room of the temple, an angel came to talk with him. Zechariah didn't see angels every day and he was terrified. The angel said, "Don't be afraid, Zechariah. God has heard your prayers and your wife will have a son. You are to give him the name John. Many, many people will rejoice with you at his birth. Your son will be filled with the Holy Spirit and will convince many Israelites to follow God. Your son will prepare people for the coming of the Lord. He will encourage them to prepare their hearts for Him."

Zechariah was amazed at what the angel said. "How can I know this will

really happen? It seems impossible because my wife and I are both very old."

The angel said, "My name is Gabriel and I am God's messenger. He sent me to you and since you do not believe my message, you will not be able to speak until the child is born."

As this was all happening, the people were outside praying and waiting for Zechariah to come out. They didn't know he was talking to Gabriel but they wondered what was taking so long. When Zechariah did come out, he couldn't speak to them. They figured out from his motions that he had seen an angel inside the temple.

Zechariah stayed at the temple until it was time for him to leave and then he went home. Soon after he got home, his wife Elizabeth became pregnant.

The Birth of John the Baptist *Luke 1:57-66*

Zechariah was unable to speak for the whole nine months his wife was pregnant. That was exactly what the angel had said would happen. When it was time for Elizabeth and Zechariah's baby to be born all of their relatives and neighbors came to celebrate with them as was the custom. The little baby boy was born healthy and strong. When he was eight days old, there was a special ceremony during which he was to be given a name. The neighbors and relatives suggested that he be named Zechariah in honor of his father but Elizabeth said, "No, his name will be John."

"What?" they asked. "Why would you name him John? There are no men named John in your family!" They turned to Zechariah and asked his opinion on the name. They were certain Zechariah would agree with them. The old priest motioned for a tablet to write on and to everyone's amazement he wrote, "His name is John." As soon as he wrote the name his voice returned and he began praising God! Everyone who heard about this was amazed. They all wondered what this little boy would be when he grew up.

JESUS IS BORN

God gave John the Baptist the job of announcing that Jesus was coming to do God's work on Earth. His plan was to send Jesus to Earth as a human being. Jesus entered the world just as everyone does—as a baby. Jesus' birth had miracles all around it because, after all, He was leaving the royalty of Heaven behind. He didn't come to Earth in a palace just so rich people could know Him. His birth was simple, just as the prophets had predicted.

An Angel Speaks to Mary *Luke 1:26-38*

Elizabeth was six months pregnant when the same angel who had promised her a baby made a visit to a young woman named Mary. This young woman was engaged to be married to a man named Joseph. He was a carpenter and way back in his family tree was the great King David. Gabriel appeared to Mary and said, "Greetings, Mary. God is very happy with you!"

Mary was confused by this statement. She couldn't figure out what the angel meant so she was afraid. "Don't be frightened," the angel said. "God has decided to bless you in a wonderful way! He has decided that you will have a baby . . . a son whom you will name Jesus. This baby will be very great and will be the Son of God himself. God will give this child the throne of King David. He will reign over Israel forever! His kingdom will never end!"

Mary was amazed at this statement. She was also confused. "How can I have a baby?" she asked. "I'm not even married."

The angel told her that God's power would make her pregnant. "The baby you have will be the Son of God," said Gabriel. Then the angel told her that her cousin, Elizabeth, was also going to have a baby. "People used to say that she would never have a baby because she's already so old, but nothing is impossible with God."

Mary thought about everything the angel said. She thought about how much she loved God. Then she said, "I will do whatever the Lord wants. I am His servant." When the angel heard this he left her.

Jesus Is Born   *Matthew 1:18-25; Luke 2:1-7*

Right after the angel Gabriel came to tell Mary that she was going to have a baby, God's angel also visited Joseph. "Joseph, the girl you are engaged to marry is going to have a baby. But the baby she is having is God's Son. Don't be afraid to go ahead and marry her. She is a woman who has found great favor with God. When the baby is born, name Him Jesus because He will save His people from their sins." When Joseph woke up

he did exactly what the angel said; he married Mary.

A short time later, the Roman emperor decided he wanted to know how many people lived in his kingdom. To find out that number he ordered that a count of all the people in the land be taken. People had to go back to the towns their ancestors had once lived in to be counted. That meant that Joseph had to go to the city of Bethlehem where his ancestor King David had lived. Joseph left Nazareth with Mary. It was a difficult trip for Mary

because she was ready to have a baby any day.

When they arrived in Bethlehem, the little town was crowded with people who had come to be counted. Joseph had trouble finding a place for them to stay. They ended up staying in a stable because there was no room in the inn. That very night Mary gave birth to her baby. She and Joseph named Him Jesus, just as the angel had told them to do. When the little boy was born, Mary wrapped Him tightly in strips of cloth and laid Him in the animal's feedbox.

Shepherds Visit Jesus *Luke 2:8-20*

The same night that Mary gave birth to Jesus some shepherds in a field outside of Bethlehem had an interesting experience. Late that night, the shepherds were watching for animals that might hurt their sleeping sheep. The night was dark and quiet but suddenly the sky above them lit up with the presence of God's angel! The glory of God filled the whole sky so that it was as light as daytime. The shepherds were amazed when the angel spoke to them. "Do not be afraid," the angel said. "I have wonderful news for you!

God's Son has been born tonight in the little village of Bethlehem. He is your Savior, Christ the Lord. You will find Him wrapped in strips of cloth and lying in an animal's feedbox."

The shepherds were even more amazed when a whole choir of angels filled the sky. They all praised God singing, "Glory to God in the highest, and peace on Earth to all men on whom God's favor rests!"

When the angels left, the shepherds were filled with excitement. "Let's go to Bethlehem and find the baby they were talking about!" they said. So they hurried to Bethlehem and found the baby who was lying in the feedbox just as the angel said. The shepherds were amazed by this and they told everyone they met about the baby and what the angel told them about Him. Mary listened to everything they said about Jesus and she kept all these things in her heart and mind. As the shepherds returned to their work in the fields, they praised God and glorified Him for this wonderful gift.

Wise Men Visit Jesus *Matthew 2:1-12*

Sometime after Jesus was born a special star appeared in the sky over a country to the east of Judah. Some wise men saw the star and they knew that it meant a new king had been born. So the wise men packed gifts to give the king and began traveling. The star moved slowly through the sky and the wise men followed it. The star led them to Jerusalem where the wise men went to visit King Herod. "Where is the new king of the Jews?" they asked. "We saw His star in the sky and have followed it here."

King Herod was very angry to hear that there was a new king. He asked them many questions about the star and what it meant. The wise men told him what the prophets had taught about a new king of the Jews. So he told the wise men to go on to Bethlehem and look for the king there. "Please return to me and tell me where this king is so that I can go worship Him too," King Herod asked.

The star began moving again so the wise men followed it all the way to Bethlehem. The star stopped right over the little house where Jesus lived with Joseph and Mary. The wise men bowed to the young king and gave Him the gifts they had brought for Him: gold, sweet smelling frankincense, and a perfume called myrrh. When the wise men left Bethlehem they did not go back to Jerusalem to report to King Herod. God warned them in a dream to stay away from the king because he wanted to hurt the child, not worship Him.

Escape to Egypt *Matthew 2:13-23*

Not long after the wise men left, God appeared to Joseph in a dream. "Get up right now," God said, "take Mary and Jesus and get out of Judah. Run to Egypt because King Herod wants to hurt Jesus. In fact, he is going to search for the child and try to kill Him. Stay in Egypt until I tell you it is safe to come back."

Joseph went right away and got Mary and Jesus up, even though it was the middle of the night, and they escaped to Egypt. They stayed there until God came to Joseph in another dream and told him it was safe to return to Judah.

When King Herod realized that the wise men had tricked him by going home another way he was very angry! He wanted to make sure that this new king of the Jews didn't take his kingdom so he ordered that all the little boys in or near Bethlehem who were two years old or younger be killed! That would cover all the boy babies from the time the wise men had come to see him until the present. It was a terrible time. Mothers begged for their sons to be saved and sobbed and cried when they weren't.

When King Herod died, the angel of God told Joseph it was safe to take Jesus home because those who were trying to hurt Him were dead. Joseph took Mary and Jesus to Nazareth, because he heard that another bad king was ruling in the area where they had lived before. This made the prophecy true that Jesus would be called a Nazarene— one who was from Nazareth.

JESUS GROWING UP

Jesus grew up in the little village of Nazareth. Joseph was a carpenter so Jesus may have learned carpentry from him. The Bible does not give much information about Jesus' childhood. But the story of when He went to Jerusalem with His mother and father to attend the Passover Feast celebration is an important one. That trip reminded Mary and Joseph that there was something special about their son.

The Boy in the Temple *Luke 2:41-52*

Every year Jesus' parents traveled to Jerusalem for the Passover Feast celebration. The year that Jesus was 12 years old they made the trip as usual and when the feast was over the family left for home. Mary and Joseph were walking with a large group of family and friends. They assumed Jesus was somewhere in the group. They didn't know that He had actually

stayed behind in Jerusalem. After the group had been walking for a while, Mary and Joseph looked for Jesus but they couldn't find Him anywhere. They quickly turned around and went right back to Jerusalem. The worried couple looked everywhere for the young boy. They searched everywhere they had been. They searched places He might have been curious about. They looked and looked for three days but didn't find Him anywhere. Finally on the third day they found Jesus. He was in the temple with the wise and educated teachers. He was listening to them talk and asking them questions. Everyone in the temple was amazed at how wise He was and what good questions He asked. Jesus not only asked good questions, He had good answers for their questions.

Mary went right up to Jesus and asked Him, "Why did You do this? Your father and I have been very worried about You. We've been searching everywhere in the city for You!"

"Why were you searching everywhere for me?" Jesus answered. "You should have known that I would be in my Father's House." Mary and Joseph didn't understand what He meant. But Jesus went home to Nazareth with them. He obeyed them and honored them as His parents. Mary thought about this incident often as she watched Jesus grow into a young man. Everyone liked Him and He honored and obeyed God in all He did.

THE MINISTRY OF JOHN

It was a miracle that John was born to his elderly parents. But God had special work for the son of Zechariah to do. John paved the way . . . he let people know that Jesus, God's Son, was coming. John told the people to get ready to hear Jesus' message and to learn from Him!

A Strange Man *Matthew 3:1-12; Luke 3:1-16*

God gave John the Baptist a special job to do. He traveled around in the wilderness outside of towns and preached about Jesus! He told the people, "Turn away from your sins and turn to God because the kingdom of Heaven is near." The Old Testament prophet Isaiah wrote that a messenger would come ahead of God's Son and would let people know that God's Son was coming. John was that messenger.

John was an unusual man. He wore clothes made from camel's hair with a leather belt around his waist. He ate locusts and wild honey. But even though he was odd, people came from all over to hear John preach. People listened to him and confessed their sins and repented of them, then John baptized them in the Jordan River. That's how he got the name John the Baptist.

One time John saw some of the leaders of the church coming to be baptized and he knew what their hearts were like. "You are a bunch of snakes!" he said. "Show by the way you live that you have truly repented of your sins. Don't assume that you are automatically safe from God's judgment just because your ancestor was Abraham. Don't you see that God is ready to chop you off from His family? He cuts down every tree that doesn't produce fruit."

John continued with, "I baptize you with water, after you turn away from your sins, but there is One coming after me who is far greater and more powerful and important than I am. I am not even worthy to be His servant but He will baptize you with the Holy Spirit.

He will separate the useful people from those who aren't serious about knowing and serving God."

"What do we do?" the people asked. "How do we show God we're serious about this?"

"If you have two coats, give one to someone who has none," John said. "If you have food, share it with someone who has none."

Dishonest taxpayers came too, to have John baptize them. "Stop being dishonest," John told them. "Treat people fairly."

Many people listened to John and turned away from their sins and followed God.

Jesus Is Baptized

Matthew 3:13-17; Mark 1:9-11;
Luke 3:21, 22; John 1:29-34

One day John was preaching to people near the town of Bethany and baptizing many of them in the Jordan River. While he was working Jesus came up to him. "I want you to baptize me," He said.

"I can't baptize You," John said. "I am the one who should be baptized by You. Why are You asking me to do this?"

Jesus answered gently, "I must do everything in the right way. Please baptize me." So John led Jesus out into the waters of the Jordan River and he baptized Him. As John lifted Jesus up out of the water he saw the clouds above them divide and a dove flew down and settled on Jesus. It was God's Holy Spirit! Then a voice boomed from Heaven. God said, "This is my Son. I love Him very much and I'm very happy with Him!"

The next day John saw Jesus again. He pointed toward Jesus and announced to all the people near by, "Look, there is the Lamb of God who will take away all our sins! He is the One I've been talking about when I said that someone was coming who is greater and more powerful than I am. I didn't know that He was the One until I baptized Him. Then I saw the Holy Spirit come and rest on Him and a voice from Heaven said that He is God's Son! I saw this happen. I know for certain that He is the One I've been preaching about!"

John the Baptist baptized Jesus and now Jesus was ready to begin His work for God. He was about 30 years old and God had some important work for Him to do. It wasn't always going to be easy . . . in fact, the first thing that happened showed Him how difficult His work was going to be!

Jesus Is Tempted

Matthew 4:1-11; Mark 1:12, 13; Luke 4:1-13

After Jesus was baptized He left the area around the Jordan River. It was time for His work for God to begin but something else had to happen first. The Spirit of God led Him out into the wilderness where the devil met Him. They were there in the wilderness together for 40 days and 40 nights.

That whole time the devil was tempting Jesus to turn away from God. Jesus ate no food for that whole 40 days which, of course, meant that He was very hungry.

"If You are really the Son of God," the devil said, "then take these stones here on the ground and change them into bread."

"No!" Jesus said. "The Scriptures tell us that people need more than just bread to have a good life."

Then the devil took Jesus to a very high place. He showed Him all the nations of the world; all the land and all the people. "I will give You all of this to rule," the devil said. "You will have glory and power and authority over these kingdoms. I can do this because I have authority over all of them. I can give them to anyone I please. I will give it all to You if You will just bow down and worship me," he said.

"I will not because I know that the Scriptures say to worship God and God alone and to only serve Him. I will not bow down to you," Jesus answered.

The devil had one more plan. He took Jesus to the temple in Jerusalem. They went to the highest part of the building and the devil said, "If You are really God's Son then jump off. I know that the Scriptures say that God orders His angels to take care of You; so they will catch You and even keep You from hurting yourself at all."

"Yes, well the Scriptures also say that You shouldn't test the Lord your God!" Jesus said. The devil knew then that he wasn't going to make any progress with this temptation so he left . . . but he wasn't finished with Jesus.

Jesus Calls His Disciples
Matthew 4:18-22; 9:9-13;
Mark 1:14-20; 2:14-17; Luke 5:1-11; 27-32; John 1:35-51

Jesus began His ministry for God by teaching people about His Father. He challenged people to turn away from their sins and obey God. Many people followed Jesus; either because they believed Him and what He taught or because they were curious about Him. Jesus chose 12 men to be His special students. They are called Jesus' disciples. Most of the

253

men He called to follow Him were fishermen. Some He saw working on their nets and He called them to follow Him. One time He was teaching some people as He stood on the shore of a lake. The crowd of people pressed in on Him so He was nearly pushed into the water. Jesus saw a couple of fishing boats nearby so He climbed into one of them and taught the crowd from there. The fishermen were a little ways off washing their nets after working all night. When Jesus was finished teaching the people, He told the fisherman (who owned the boat He was sitting in) to push the boat out into deeper water where he would catch a lot of fish.

"Sir, we worked hard for the whole

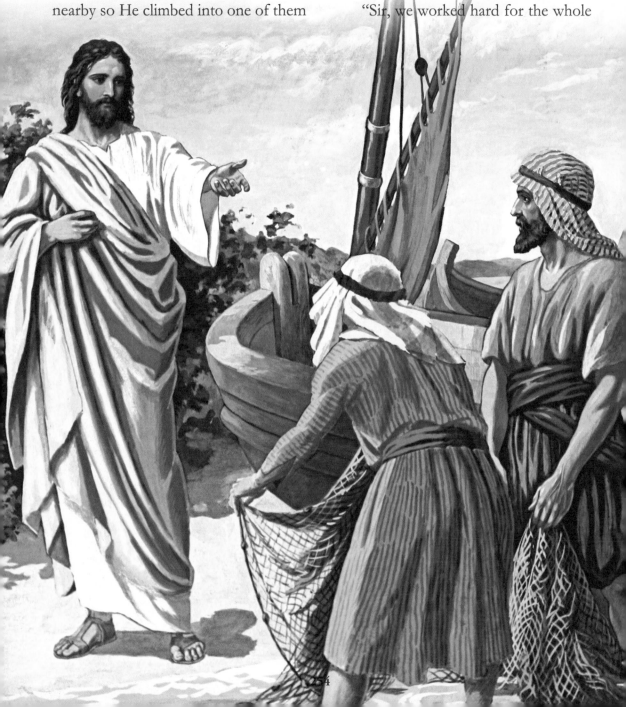

night," the fisherman named Simon said. "We fished in that very spot but we didn't catch even one fish. Our nets are all clean now, so why should we go out to that same spot?" Jesus just looked at Simon until the fisherman finally gave in and pushed the boat out into the water and dropped his nets. Immediately the nets were filled with so many fish that Simon had to call for help in order to pull the nets up. Simon was amazed. He realized that Jesus was no ordinary man. "I'm too much of a sinner to be around You. Please leave me!" Simon begged.

"Don't be afraid," Jesus said. "Follow me and I'll show you how to fish for people!" Simon left his boat right there and followed Jesus.

Another time, Jesus saw a tax collector sitting in his booth collecting tax money from the people. The people hated tax collectors because many of them were dishonest and collected extra money to keep for themselves. But Jesus turned to this tax collector, named Matthew, and said, "Come and follow me!" Matthew got up right away and followed Him. Later Matthew hosted a big banquet for many of his tax collector friends and Jesus attended it too.

The religious leaders criticized Jesus for being with the hated tax collectors. But Jesus said, "Healthy people are not the ones who need a doctor; sick people need doctors. I have come to challenge sinners to stop sinning and that is why I spend time with sinners. I don't want to spend time with people who believe they are already good enough for God."

Jesus finished calling His 12 special disciples. Their names were Peter, Andrew (Peter's brother); James, John, Philip, Bartholomew, Matthew, Thomas, James, Simon, Judas, and Judas Iscariot.

JESUS' MINISTRY BEGINS

The preparation was done. Jesus experienced what it felt like to be truly tempted to turn away from God. He began teaching about obeying God and had many people following Him. He also had chosen His 12 special students who would be with Him every step of the way. Now it was time to take His ministry and work to the next level. Big things were about to happen!

A Wedding in Cana *John 2:1-11*

Mary, Jesus' mother, was invited to a wedding celebration in the town of Cana. Jesus and His disciples were invited to the wedding too. Wedding celebrations went on for days and days. It was a big party for many people! Part way through this celebration though, there was a problem. The host of the party ran out of wine. Wine was the main beverage for the party and it would be a disgrace for the host to run out before the party was over. Mary heard that the host had this problem and she wanted to help him. The only thing Mary could think of was to go to her Son. So she pulled Jesus aside and told Him, "They have no more wine."

"That's too bad," Jesus said. "But I can't do anything about it. The time for me to do miracles hasn't come yet."

But Mary just ignored what He said.

She turned to some servants standing nearby and instructed them to do whatever Jesus told them to do.

There were six large stone pitchers nearby. They were big pitchers that each held 20 or 30 gallons of water but they were empty at the moment. Jesus pointed to the pitchers and told the servants to fill them up with water. When the pitchers were all filled, Jesus told a servant to dip out some of the water and take it to the host of the celebration.

When the man tasted what the servant brought him, he was amazed! It was no longer water. It was the most delicious and most expensive wine he had ever tasted. He didn't know where it had come from (although the servant knew). The host called the bridegroom over and said, "Usually people serve the best wine first and then cheaper wine later. But you have definitely saved the best for last!"

Of course the bridegroom had no idea what the man was talking about. He didn't know that Jesus had just performed the first miracle of His ministry on Earth by changing the water into wine. When the disciples saw what Jesus did they believed that He was a special man and that the power of God was with Him!

Jesus Clears the Temple *John 2:13-25*

It was time for the annual Passover Celebration so Jesus went to Jerusalem. It was the custom for people to come to the temple and offer sacrifices to God. But when Jesus came into the temple He saw merchants selling cattle, sheep, and doves. The people were buying the animals so they had sacrifices to offer. But the merchants were charging very high prices to the poor people. Jesus was angry that these merchants were making a profit from the poor people who just wanted to honor God.

Jesus grabbed some ropes and made a whip out of them. He snapped the whip and chased the merchants out of the temple and scattered the animals. Then He turned over the tables of the moneychangers who were cheating the people too. He shouted, "Get out of here! Do not turn my Father's house into a den of thieves!"

The temple leaders got very angry at Him. "What right do You have to come in here and do these things? If You truly have the authority from God to do this, then show us some miraculous sign!"

Jesus answered, "Fine! Destroy this temple and I will raise it back up again in three days!"

"What are You talking about?" the Jewish leaders asked. "It took 46 years to build this temple and You think You can do it in three days?" They didn't understand that Jesus was not talking about the temple building. He was talking about His own body. He was saying that His body would be raised back to life three days after He died. His disciples remembered this after He was actually raised from the dead and they believed in Him and in the Scriptures.

Because of the miracles Jesus did in Jerusalem during the Passover many people believed that He was the Messiah.

A very important part of Jesus' ministry was that He taught others how to know God better and how to live for Him. It was important to Jesus that people obey God and be honest about their faith in Him. Jesus taught important lessons and sometimes explained them with interesting stories. Jesus made sure that the people who needed to learn about God's love could understand His lessons. He didn't worry much about the religious leaders who already thought they knew everything.

The Sermon on the Mount *Matthew 5–6:4*

Large crowds of people followed Jesus everywhere He went. One day Jesus led His followers up on a mountain where He sat down with them and taught important lessons. Jesus taught His followers that God blesses people who think of others before themselves. He blesses people who are peaceful and those who take a stand for their faith in God.

Jesus taught that people who believe in God are like salt that flavors food or keeps food from spoiling. People who believe in God are like lights in a dark place. Jesus said that it wouldn't be right to cover a light so that it couldn't light a room. In the same way it isn't right to hide your faith in God so that others can't see it.

Jesus also taught lessons about anger. He said that people who can't control their anger are subject to being judged by God. "So," Jesus said, "if you are angry with someone or know that someone is angry with you, go talk with them and get it settled as quickly as possible. Don't bother coming to God and asking Him for things before you take care of these anger problems."

Other lessons Jesus taught were about being pure and about keeping promises and about not seeking revenge against people who hurt you. Some people believed the old saying, "an eye for an eye" so when someone hurt them they wanted to get even. Jesus said to leave all revenge to God.

Jesus also taught about loving your enemies. Everyone loves their friends, but only someone who has God's love in his heart can love people who hurt him. That's real love.

One important topic Jesus covered in this sermon was about taking care of the poor. It is important to help those who are needy. But Jesus said it is important to do helpful things in private, not in front of other people so that they will think good things about you.

How to Pray and Stand Strong

Matthew 6:5–7:29

Another part of the Sermon on the Mount was when Jesus taught about prayer. He taught that prayer is a very important part of knowing God. He even gave an example of what a good prayer sounds like. That example is now called The Lord's Prayer. It teaches us to praise God, confess our sin, and ask God for what we need.

Much of what Jesus taught about living a life of following God was how to treat other people. Jesus taught that it is important to be helpful to others, to be kind, and not to judge others. Praying for others is important too. Jesus said to keep praying, keep asking, and keep believing that God will answer. The Golden Rule He taught is to treat other people the way you would like them to treat you.

Some people worry a lot about what they are going to wear or what they will have to eat. Jesus said not to worry but to trust God. They can know God will take care of them because He takes care of the flowers and of all the animals. If He takes care of these things you can know He will also take care of you.

Knowing all of the things Jesus taught is important, because how a person lives shows that her faith in God is real. God is serious about who will be called His child. The pathway that leads to Heaven is clearly described by God. You can't just live any way you want. It's important to live the way He says. If you do, your life will show kindness and concern for others.

Jesus gave an example of how important it is to believe His teachings. He said that a man who builds his house on a rock is smart because his house will stand firm in all kinds of storms. But a man who builds his house on sand will have problems when the storms come and wash the house away. Believing Jesus' teachings is like building your house on rock. You can stand strong because you are living the right way!

The Lord's Prayer

Our Father which art in heaven, Hallowed be thy name. Thy kingdom come. Thy will be done in earth, as it is in heaven.

Give us this day our daily bread. And forgive us our debts as we forgive our debtors. And lead us not into temptation, but deliver us from evil: For thine is the kingdom, and the power, and the glory, forever.

Amen.

Jesus Talks with Nicodemus *John 3:1-21*

Late one night a man named Nicodemus came to see Jesus. Nicodemus was a Pharisee—a religious leader. He didn't want any of the other religious leaders to know that he was talking with Jesus. He had important things that he wanted to discuss with Jesus. "We have all seen the miracles You do," Nicodemus said. "We know that God is with You."

Jesus said, "I want you to know that you cannot enter God's kingdom unless you are born again."

"I don't know what You mean," Nicodemus said. "How can I go back into my mother's body and be born again?"

"No, that isn't what I mean," Jesus said. "Humans can only give birth to other humans. But the Holy Spirit can give life from Heaven. That's the kind of birth I'm talking about."

"I don't understand," Nicodemus said.

"You are a Jewish religious teacher and you don't understand what I'm saying?" Jesus asked. "I am telling you that I am the Son of Man and I have come to Earth so that people may have eternal life. God loved the world so much that He sent His only Son to Earth so that everyone who believes in Him can be saved and have eternal life. Those who believe will not have judgment in their future. But those who do not believe will be judged. Their judgment is based on the fact that they had the light of the world right in front of them and yet they didn't believe. They hate the light because they want to live in the darkness and do the sins that are part of that life. Those who want to do what is right come into the light and do what God wants."

The Woman at the Well *John 4:1-38*

One time Jesus and His disciples were walking to Galilee. They cut through a part of the country called Samaria. Jesus was tired from the long walk so He sat beside a well to rest while His disciples went into town to get some food. While Jesus was sitting there, a woman came to the well to get some water. Jesus asked her for a drink of water. The woman was surprised that He spoke to her. Most Jews wouldn't have anything to do with Samaritans. They thought they were better than the lowly Samaritans. "You are a Jew and I am a Samaritan. Why are You asking me for water?" she asked.

"If you only knew who I really am, you would be asking me for living water," Jesus said.

"You don't have a rope or a bucket," the woman said. "This is a very deep well. How are You going to get water? Besides, do You think Your water is better than the water in this well that our ancestor Jacob dug?"

"People get thirsty again after they drink this water," Jesus said. "But the water I give takes away thirst altogether. They will never be thirsty again."

"Please give me some of that water," the woman said. "Then I'll never have to come to this well again."

"OK, go get your husband," Jesus said.

"I don't have a husband," the woman answered.

"That's right, you do not," Jesus said, "but you have had five husbands. And the man you are with right now is not your husband."

"You must be a prophet," the woman said. "So tell me why you Jews insist that we worship in Jerusalem but we think it is OK to worship here where our ancestors worshiped."

"The time is coming when it won't matter where you worship," Jesus said. "God is looking for those who will worship Him in spirit and in truth."

"I don't know what You are talking about," the woman said. "When the Messiah comes then all this religious talk will make sense."

"I am the Messiah," Jesus said.

Just then His disciples returned with the food. They were surprised to see Him talking with the woman from Samaria. The woman left her water jar right there beside the well and ran into the town. "Come with me!" she called to everyone she met. "Come with me to the well. The Messiah is there. I know that He is the Messiah because He told me everything I have ever done."

Meanwhile the disciples tried to give Jesus food but He wouldn't eat. "I have food to eat that you don't know about," He told them. "My nourishment comes from doing the will of God," He said.

Mary and Martha *Luke 10:38-42*

One time Jesus and His disciples were on the way to Jerusalem. They stopped to visit some good friends in Bethany. They were two sisters who lived together and they were named Mary and Martha. As soon as Jesus and His friends came into the house, Mary sat right down at Jesus' feet and began talking with Him. She loved listening to Him teach and asking Him questions. But Martha didn't take time to talk with Jesus. She was busy preparing dinner and worrying over making everything perfect. After a while, Martha got frustrated that Mary wasn't helping her with the kitchen work. She went to Jesus and said, "Don't You think it is unfair that Mary is making me do all the work? Tell her to come help me in the kitchen!"

"My dear Martha," Jesus said. "You are worrying too much about the dinner and all the preparations. These details don't matter to me. Stop worrying about things. Mary knows that talking with me is the most important thing. I'm not going to tell her to help you. No, I want you to come and talk with me!"

The Story of the Sower

Matthew 13:1-23; Mark 4:13-30; Luke 8:4-15

Jesus had a special lesson in mind when He taught this story to His followers:

A farmer went out to plant some seed. He took a handful of the seed and began scattering it on the ground. Some of the seed landed on a sidewalk and birds swooped down and ate up those seeds. Other seed landed on soil that wasn't very deep and beneath that soil was a thick layer of rock. The seed took root and plants began growing, but when the sun got hot they wilted and died. Since the soil was not very deep there wasn't enough food and water for the roots of the plants—that is why they died. Other seed landed in the middle of a lot of weeds. Those plants tried to grow but the weeds were stronger so they took all the food and water away from the plants. The weeds grew strong and the plants died. However, some of the seeds fell on good soil. Those seeds grew into plants that were strong and healthy. They produced a wonderful crop that was better than the farmer ever dreamed it could be.

When Jesus finished the story, His disciples came and asked Him, "Why do You always tell stories when You talk to the people?"

Jesus answered, "You have been given the gift of understanding the things of God's kingdom and you are blessed because of that. But not everyone does understand. Some people will never understand because they are too stubborn. But for those who want to understand, it helps to have stories that explain the meaning."

Then Jesus explained the meaning of the story He had just told. "The seed in this story represents the truth about God's kingdom. The seed that fell on the sidewalk represents those who hear the truth about God's kingdom but don't understand it. The devil comes and snatches that truth away, just as the birds in the story quickly ate the farmer's seed. The shallow soil represents those people who hear the message of God's love and accept it. But their roots don't go very deep because they don't trust God and learn more about Him. Then when they have problems they turn away from Him. The ground with lots of weeds represents people who accept God's Word and trust Him, but they try to keep other things important in their lives too. These things choke out God's presence in their lives. The good soil is, of course, those who receive God's message, trust Him, love Him, and grow strong in Him. Their lives are healthy examples of God's presence in them."

The Lost Sheep *Matthew 18:12-14; Luke 15:4-7*

Another story that Jesus told was about shepherds. A lot of people who listened to Jesus teach were shepherds so they had a special understanding of this story.

Jesus said, "Suppose a shepherd had 100 sheep in his flock. Of course, every one of those sheep is important to him. So if one sheep wanders away and is lost, the shepherd will be worried. He knows that a sheep that isn't with the rest of the flock is in danger of being attacked by a wild animal or of getting hurt. The shepherd will leave the other 99 sheep alone while he goes and looks for that one sheep. That's how important that one sheep is to him. When he finds the lost sheep he will celebrate and tell everyone who will listen how happy he is! He is probably happier about finding that one sheep than he is about the 99 sheep who didn't wander away. This story shows you how happy God is when one lost sinner comes to Him. He celebrates every person who turns away from evil to follow Him. That's because He doesn't want even one person to die without knowing Him."

The Lost Coin *Luke 15:8-10*

After Jesus told the story of the lost sheep, He made the same point again in another story. "There was a woman who owned 10 very valuable coins. Her 10 coins were worth a lot of money. One day she lost one of her coins. She looked everywhere in her little house for that coin. She looked in drawers and under furniture. She looked in all her pockets and everywhere she could think of. She could not find the lost coin anywhere. She lit all the lamps in her house and swept every corner of every room. The coin was no where to be found. But finally, almost when she had given up, she found the coin in the most unlikely of places! The woman was overjoyed! She danced and sang and told everyone she could find that she had found her lost coin. She called in friends and neighbors to celebrate with her because the coin that was lost was now found!"

Jesus said, "Notice how happy the woman was to find her lost coin. In that same way, God rejoices over every single person who comes to Him. Even His angels celebrate when someone comes to faith in Christ!"

The Vine and the Branches *John 15:1-17*

Another time Jesus was talking with His disciples when one of them asked Him questions about why He was teaching His followers so much but not explaining things to everyone. Jesus gave them an illustration about His relationship with them. He called himself the True Vine and explained things this way . . . "I am the true vine and God, my Father, is the gardener. As He cares for the plants in His garden, He cuts off the branches of the plants that do not bear fruit because they are useless. Even the branches that do grow fruit have to be pruned. That means He cuts them back just a little because that keeps them healthier. You, as branches of my vine, are pruned by hearing my teachings. Stay close to me and I will stay close to you. Remember that a branch cannot grow fruit if it is cut off from the vine that provides it food and water. In the same way, you can't be fruitful if you are not connected to me. Without me you can do nothing. So, if you cut off your relationship to me, you will end up being thrown away because you are useless. Stay close to me, study my words, know me, and your prayers will be answered. My followers produce good fruit and that brings my Father joy!

"I love you all just as my Father loves me. Keep obeying my teachings just as I obey my Father. I want you to be filled with the joy of obeying and knowing my Father! Please, please, love each other. Don't let anything get in the way of that love. Real love would do anything for others; anything at all. You are truly my friends and that is why I have told you all these things. You are chosen to live in such a way that you grow fruit for my Father's kingdom. Start that by loving one another!"

A Run Away Son *Luke 15:11-32*

J esus told another story about how God celebrates when people who don't know Him come to Him. It went like this: There once was a man who had two sons. The younger son didn't like working in the fields. He went to his father and said, "I know that when you die I will get a share of your wealth. Give me my inheritance now so that I can go live on my own. I don't want to wait until you die." The father may have felt sad about his son's decision, but he went ahead and gave him his share of the inheritance.

278

The boy took the money and packed up his things and headed out. He spent the money as fast as he could. Pretty soon he had wasted all the money on wild parties and foolish things. About the same time that the boy's money ran out, a famine hit the land and it was hard to find food anywhere. The boy got very hungry but couldn't find any food. Finally the boy convinced a farmer to give him a job feeding his pigs.

The boy was so hungry that even the pigs' food looked good to him! But he couldn't find any food for himself and no one would give him any.

After a while the boy realized that he had made a mistake by leaving his father's house. He thought, "Even the men who work for my father have food to eat and here I am starving to death. Maybe I'll go home and ask my father for a job. I'll tell him that I know I don't

279

deserve to be called his son anymore but I will beg him for a job."

So the boy started for home. He was still quite a distance from his father's house when his father saw him coming. His father had been waiting for the boy to come back home and he was filled with love for his long-lost son. He ran to him and gave him the biggest hug ever! The young boy said, "Father,

I have sinned against you. I'm not worthy of being called your son anymore."

But his father didn't pay any attention to what the boy said. He called his servants and told them, "Get busy! Bring the finest robe we have and put it on my son. Put rings on his fingers and sandals on his feet. Prepare a big feast. We are going to have a party because my son that was lost has now come home!"

In the meantime, the farmer's older son was out working in the fields. He didn't know that his brother had come home. But when he came back to the house at the end of the day he saw all the party preparations and smelled the wonderful dinner that had been cooked. He asked one of the servants what was happening and was told that his brother had come home. The servant told him that his father had ordered a big party

to be prepared. The older son got angry about this and went to find his father. "Why are you throwing a big party for my brother? He took your money and wasted it on foolish living. I've been here working hard for you the whole time he was in the city wasting your money. I've never once refused to do what you asked me to do. And you have never thrown a party for me; in fact, you never did anything for me. Now this boy comes home after all his foolish living and you throw him a feast? That isn't fair!"

The father was sad that his son felt this way. He said, "Look, my son. You and I are very close and I share everything with you. But we have to celebrate this day because I thought your brother was dead but now he is here! He was lost and now he is found!"

The Unforgiving Debtor *Matthew 18:21-35*

One time Peter asked Jesus a question that he had been thinking about for a while. "How often should I forgive someone who sins against me? Is seven times enough?"

"No," Jesus said. "Seventy times seven is closer to the answer! For this

very reason the kingdom of Heaven can be compared to a king who decided to collect the money owed to him by some of his servants. Things were going along well until one servant came forward who owed the king millions of dollars. The servant did not have the money to pay his debt so the king ordered that the man's wife and children and everything the man owned be sold and the money be given to the king. The man begged the king for mercy. He promised that if the king would just be a little more patient with him he would pay the debt. The king felt sorry for the man and agreed to cancel his debt.

When that man left the king's palace he went straight to another servant who owed him a few thousand dollars. He grabbed that man by the neck and shouted, 'Pay me the money you owe me right now!' The man fell down on the ground and begged for a little more time to come up with the money. But the first man would not give him any more time. He had the man arrested and thrown in jail.

Some of the other servants saw what happened. They knew that the first man had been granted mercy from the king for his own debt. They were surprised by what he did to the man who owed him money. So the servants went to the king and told him the whole story. The king called for the man whose debt he had forgiven, 'Come to see me right now!' When the man arrived the king said, 'I forgave the huge debt you owed me. Then I hear that you had another man thrown in jail who owed you less than you owed me. You did this even though he begged you for mercy. Why couldn't you show him the same kindness I showed you?' Then the king had the man thrown into prison until he could pay back every penny he owed."

Then Jesus told Peter, "That is what my heavenly Father will do to you if you refuse to forgive others with your whole heart."

The Rich Young Man

Matthew 19:16-30; Mark 10:17-31; Luke 18:18-30

One time a man ran up to Jesus, knelt down on his knees, and asked this question, "Good Teacher, what do I have to do in order to know for certain that I have eternal life?"

"Why do you call me good?" Jesus answered. "Only God is truly good. To answer your question, I remind you of the commandments. They say, 'Do not murder. Do not commit adultery. Do not steal. Do not lie. Do not cheat. Honor your father and mother.'"

"I have kept all these commandments since the time I was very young," the man said.

Jesus felt a real love for the young man so He said, "You are only missing one thing. Sell everything that you own and give the money to the poor and you will have a great treasure in Heaven. Then come and follow me."

But the young man was very wealthy and he didn't want to sell his things. He sadly walked away from Jesus.

Jesus watched the young man leave, then He said to His disciples, "It is very hard for a rich man to get into God's kingdom." The disciples were surprised to hear Him say that. He continued, "It is easier for a camel to walk through the eye of a needle than it is for a rich man to enter Heaven."

"Well, if the rich can't be saved, then who can?" the disciples asked.

"If you depend on human strength then it is impossible. But with God all things are possible," Jesus said.

"Jesus, we have given up everything—our jobs and our families—to follow You," Peter said.

"I promise you," Jesus said, "that those who have given up everything—family, homes, and jobs—to follow me will receive a hundred times more. But they will also have to endure persecutions. But in the future they will have eternal life. Those people who think they are so important right now will be the least important in the future and the least important now will be the most important then."

A Woman Gives Everything

Mark 12:41-44; Luke 21:1-4

J esus and His disciples went into the temple. He sat down near the box where people came to give their offerings. There were some rich people who came into the temple and put large amounts of money in the offering. They were proud of the large offerings they gave. Then a poor woman, who was a widow, came to give her offering. She dropped only two pennies in the box. But Jesus noticed her gift and He called His disciples to come to Him. He said, "That woman who just put two pennies in the box has given more than any of the rich people. They all gave a tiny part of all the money they have. But this woman gave everything she has."

The Good Samaritan *Luke 10:25-37*

A man who was an expert in religious law came to talk with Jesus one day. He asked, "What do I have to do to get eternal life?"

"What does Moses' law say?" asked Jesus.

"It says to love God with all my heart, soul, strength, and mind," the man answered. "Then it says to love my neighbor in the same way I love myself."

"Do that and you will have eternal life," Jesus said.

"Well, exactly who is my neighbor?" the man asked.

Jesus told a story to answer the man's question. "There was a Jewish man who took a trip from Jericho to Jerusalem. As he was walking robbers attacked him. They stripped his clothes off. They took his money and beat him up then left him bleeding by the side of the road. He was nearly dead.

A little while later a Jewish priest came down that same road. He saw the poor

man lying on the side of the road. But instead of helping the man, he crossed the road and hurried on his way. Later, a man who worked in the temple came along. He saw the hurt man too. But he didn't help him either. He also crossed the road and went on his way.

A Samaritan man was the next person to come down the road. Now, Jews and Samaritans don't get along with each other very well, but when the Samaritan saw the poor man lying there in a pool of blood, he felt bad for him. The Samaritan picked up the man and put him on his own donkey and took him to an inn. He washed the man's wounds and bandaged him up. The next day he gave the innkeeper some money and said, "I have to go on with my trip, but please take care of this man until he is well. If it costs more than this I will pay you when I come back through this way."

"Now," Jesus said, "which of these men acted like a real neighbor?"

"The one who helped the hurt man," the religious leader said.

"Right. Now go and do the same thing," Jesus said.

The Story of the Talents

Matthew 25:14-30; Luke 19:11-27

J esus taught about what the kingdom of Heaven is like. He said to think of it like a man who is going on a trip. Before he left town, the man called his servants together and gave them some of his own money to invest for him. He gave the first servant five bags of gold, the second servant two bags, and the third servant one bag of gold. Then he left on his trip.

The servant who had five bags of gold invested it right away and soon had doubled his master's money. The one who had two bags got busy and doubled his money too. But the one who had one bag dug a hole in his yard and buried the money.

After a long time the master returned and called the servants to him to report on what they had done with the money. The first servant brought 10 bags of gold to his master and showed that he had doubled the money. "Good job! You have been trusted with a little responsibility and have done well; now I will give you more responsibilities. Let's celebrate!" The second servant brought four bags of gold to the master. "Good job," the master said, "you have been trusted with a little responsibility and have done well; now I will give you more responsibilities. Let's celebrate!"

Finally, the third servant brought the one bag that he had buried in the yard. "I know that you are a hard master," he said, "and I was afraid to take a chance with your money so I hid it to keep it safe."

The master wasn't happy with him. "So you think I'm a hard master and that's why you hid my money? You should have at least put it in the bank so it would be collecting interest. Take the bag of money from this servant and give it to the man who has 10 bags of gold. Those who use well what they are given will be trusted with even more! But those who are not trustworthy will lose what they do have. Now get this useless servant out of my sight!"

JESUS TEACHES BY HEALING

Jesus' tender care for hurting people showed in the many times He healed people who were sick or injured. His reputation as a healer spread and people began bringing their sick friends and neighbors to be healed by Jesus. As often as He could, Jesus healed people. And sometimes He even went the next step and raised someone from the dead. These miracles showed God's loving heart and His amazing power!

Jesus Heals a Blind Man *John 9:1-34*

Jesus and His disciples were walking along a road one day when they saw a man who was blind. The man had never been able to see because he was born blind. His disciples stopped and looked at the man then they asked Jesus a question. "Master, why was this man born blind? Was it because of his sins or those of his parents?"

"He wasn't born blind because of sin at all," Jesus answered. "It was so that God's power could be seen in him. All of us need to carry out God's work while we're here because the time is short. While I am here in this world I am the light of the world."

Then Jesus bent down and spit into the dirt. He made mud and spread the mud over the blind man's eyes. Then He said, "Go wash the mud off in the Pool of Siloam." The man did what Jesus told him to do and when he came back he could see!

The people who had known him were amazed. "Is this the same man who has been blind his whole life?" they asked each other. "Why can he see now?" they wondered. Some even thought that it must be a different man, but he sure looked like the blind man they had always known.

The man kept telling them, "It's me! It's really me!"

"Who healed you?" they asked. "Why can you see now?"

He explained to them about Jesus putting the mud on his eyes and telling him to wash it off; he could see after that. They wanted to know where Jesus went but the man didn't know. So they took the man to see the Pharisees. It just so happened that Jesus healed the man on the Sabbath and the Pharisees did not approve of that since no work was to be done on that day. When the Pharisees asked the man about what had happened to him, he explained the entire story to them.

Some of the Pharisees said, "Jesus cannot be from God or He wouldn't be doing work on the Sabbath." But others wondered how an ordinary man could do such an amazing miracle. So the

Pharisees didn't agree with each other. They asked the man again what had happened and once again he told them the story. Then they asked him who he thought Jesus was.

"I guess he is a prophet," the man answered.

The Pharisees did not want to believe that Jesus had performed a miracle. Then they went to talk to the man's

294

parents. "Was your son really born blind?" they asked. "If so, why can he see now?"

"Yes, he was born blind," they answered. "We do not know why he can see now. We do not know who healed him. But he is an adult and can speak for himself so talk with him about it." They were afraid the Pharisees would kick them out of the temple if they even hinted that Jesus might be the Messiah.

So the Pharisees went back to the man and asked him the same questions. Once again, he answered in the same way. Then he asked, "Why do you keep asking me the same questions? Do you want to become Jesus' disciples too?" That really made them angry!

"We know that God spoke to Moses and we follow his teachings. We don't know where this Jesus came from."

"Well," the man said, "no one has ever been able to open the eyes of a blind man and God doesn't do what sinners tell Him to do. So He must be from God."

The Pharisees threw the man out of the temple.

Down Through the Roof

Matthew 9:1-7; Mark 2:1-12; Luke 5:18-25

Jesus came to the city of Capernaum and a large crowd gathered at the house where He was staying. Some people wanted to hear Jesus teach about God. Some were just curious about Him. Some of the religious leaders were there just to keep an eye on Him. Very soon the house was so full that not even one more person could get in. Jesus began teaching about God. Outside the house four men came up. They each were holding a corner of a cot that carried a friend of theirs who was paralyzed. They wanted Jesus to heal their friend. Since the house was so crowded they couldn't even get inside the door. The friends carried the cot up to the roof of the house, dug a hold in the roof all the way through to the room, and lowered their friend's cot down into the room. He came down right in front of Jesus. Seeing the extreme faith of these four friends, Jesus spoke to the paralyzed man, "Son, your sins are forgiven."

The religious leaders in the room were furious. "How can He forgive sins?" they asked. "What gives Him the right to do that? Only God can forgive sins."

Jesus knew what they were thinking so He said, "Is it easier to say, 'Pick up your mat and walk?' or to say, 'Your sins are forgiven?' I will prove that I have the authority to forgive sins." Then he turned to the paralyzed man again and said, "Get up. Pick up your cot and go home. You are healed."

Right away the man jumped up and picked up his own cot and pushed his way through the crowd of people in the room. The people were amazed. They said, "We've never seen anything like this!"

The Son of a Government Official

John 4:46-54

J esus traveled from town to town, teaching and challenging people to follow God. He also healed sick people and did other miracles. His very first miracle happened in Cana when He changed water to wine at a wedding party. There was a man in a nearby city who worked in the government. He was important and powerful. The man had a son who was very sick and when he heard that Jesus was in town he came to see Him. He begged

Jesus to come to Capernaum with him to heal his son. The boy was so sick that he was very near death.

Jesus said, "Do I have to keep doing miracles in order for you people to believe in me?"

"Please, please," the official said, "please come with me before my son dies!"

Jesus said, "Go on home. Your son will be fine." The man believed Jesus and started home.

While the official was on his way his servants came and met him. They told him that his son was better so he shouldn't worry. He asked them when the little boy had begun to improve. They told him, "About one o'clock yesterday his fever suddenly disappeared."

The man realized that was the exact time that Jesus had told him, "Go on home. Your son will be fine." Right then the officer and everyone in his house believed in Jesus.

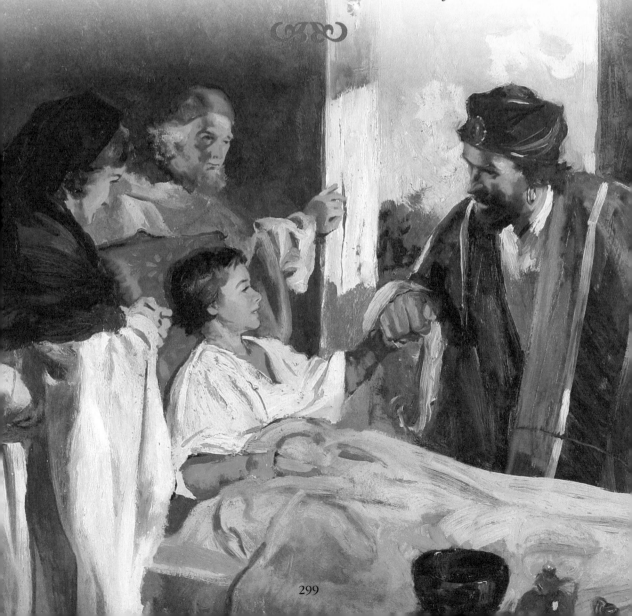

The Servant of a Roman Officer

Matthew 8:5-13; Luke 7:1-10

An officer in the Roman army came to Jesus one time and begged for His help. "Sir, my servant is paralyzed. He can't get out of bed and he is in terrible pain. Please help him."

"Alright," Jesus said, "I will come to your house with you and help him."

"I am not worthy of having You come to my house," the officer said. "Just say the word right now and I know that my servant will be healed. I understand about authority because I am under the authority of my superiors and I have people under my authority. I only need to tell them to do something and they do it."

Jesus was amazed at the faith this man had in Him. He said, "I have never seen faith like this in all of Israel." Then He turned to the Roman officer and said, "Go on home. You believed that I would heal your servant and I have done so." The officer found out later that the servant was healed right at that moment!

Jesus Heals Ten Men *Luke 17:11-37*

J esus was walking to Jerusalem. In Bible times most people walked everywhere they went. As usual, a large crowd of people was walking with Jesus. Just as the crowd crossed the border between Galilee and Samaria, Jesus noticed a group of men standing some distance away. They all suffered from the disease of leprosy. It was very contagious, so the law stated that when a person had it, he had to leave his home and live in a leper colony. That meant the sick people could not live at home with their families. This group that Jesus noticed was a group of 10 men who all had leprosy. When they saw that Jesus had noticed them, all 10 of them began shouting to Him, "Please, Jesus, have mercy on us!"

Jesus calmly told them to go and show themselves to the priests. The men may not have understood why Jesus said to do that, but they all took off running toward the temple. As they were running, their bodies were miraculously healed of the leprosy! Completely healed!

One of the men stopped right in his tracks when he realized that he was healed. He turned around and came back to Jesus, fell down on his knees, and said, "Praise God! I'm healed!" He put his face right down on the ground and just kept thanking Jesus for healing him. This particular man wasn't even a Jew. He was a Samaritan.

Of course Jesus was thankful for the man's gratitude, but He said, "Didn't I heal 10 men? Where are the other nine? Why is it just this Samaritan who returned to thank me? Where are the nine Jewish men?" Then Jesus told the man to get up off the ground and go home because his faith had made him well.

Lazarus *John 11:1-44*

Jesus had a very good friend in Bethany. His name was Lazarus and he had two sisters, Mary and Martha. When Lazarus got very sick, his sisters sent a message to Jesus asking Him to come to their home.

But when Jesus got the message He said, "Lazarus won't die from this illness. It is for God's glory." Even though Jesus loved Lazarus and his sisters very much, He didn't go to Bethany right away. He waited about two days then said, "Let's go to Judea " (that's where Bethany was).

His disciples didn't think it was a good idea to go to Judea. "Master, don't You remember that the religious leaders in Judea threatened to kill You just a few days ago? It isn't safe to go there."

"Our friend Lazarus is sleeping. We must go there and wake him," Jesus answered.

"Wait a minute," the disciples said, "if he is sleeping then that means he is getting better from his sickness." They thought Jesus was saying that Lazarus was resting, but He was actually saying that Lazarus had died.

"I am trying to tell you that Lazarus has died. I'm actually glad that I wasn't

there to help him because now you will see God's power and believe in me," Jesus said.

They all left for Bethany and when they got there Jesus was told that Lazarus had died and been buried four days before. Many friends and neighbors were at Mary and Martha's house offering their support and sympathy. Someone told Martha that Jesus was coming down the road and she ran out to meet Him. Mary stayed at home with the other people. Martha ran up to Jesus and said, "Lord, if You had been here my brother would not have died. Still, I know that God will do whatever You ask."

"Your brother will rise again," Jesus said.

"Yes, I know that when everyone rises at the resurrection he will rise too," Martha said.

"I am the resurrection and the life," Jesus said. "People who believe in me will live forever, even though they die. They will have eternal life for believing in me. Do you believe this, Martha?"

"Yes, I do believe," Martha said. "I have always believed that You are the Messiah, the Son of God." Then she went back home to her sister. "Mary, Jesus is here and He wants to see you," she told Mary. Immediately Mary went to Jesus.

"My brother would not have died if You had come," Mary said to Jesus. She began to cry and when Jesus saw her grief He was very upset. Some of the people wondered why Jesus hadn't come and helped Lazarus because they knew He could do miracles. He had healed blind people before.

"Where have you buried him?" Jesus asked. Someone told Him where Lazarus was buried and Jesus began to cry. He approached the tomb where Lazarus was buried and said, "Roll the stone away!"

"No, don't!" Martha said. "He's been buried for four days and will smell terrible!"

"I told you that you would see God's glory if you believed, didn't I?" Jesus said. So some of the men rolled the stone aside. Jesus looked up to Heaven and said, "Father, thank You for hearing my prayers." Then He shouted, "Lazarus, come out!" All the people there were amazed when Lazarus walked out of the tomb, still wrapped in the burial cloths. Jesus said, "Unwrap him and let him go!"

Jesus Calms the Storm

Matthew 8:23-27; Mark 4:35-41; Luke 8:22-25

Everywhere Jesus went a large crowd of people followed Him. He spent His days teaching them, healing them, and talking with them. He got very little rest. One day, He had been teaching all day and at evening time He said to His disciples, "Let's cross to the other side of this lake." So they all got into a boat and began sailing across the lake. Some of the people in the crowd got into other boats and followed them.

Jesus went to the back of the boat and lay down. He was so tired from the long day of teaching that He fell asleep. When the boat got out to the middle of the lake a terrible storm suddenly blew in. The wind blew the boat around and the waves crashed against it. The disciples were terrified. They thought they were going to die out there on the lake! They frantically went to Jesus and said, "Teacher, help us! We're going to drown out here!"

Jesus got up and looked at the waves, "Be still!" He said. Immediately the wind stopped blowing and the waves calmed down. Everything was quiet. Then Jesus turned to His disciples and asked, "Why were you so afraid? Don't you have faith in me?"

All of His disciples were amazed at Jesus' power. "Who is this man?" they asked each other. "Even the wind and waves obey Him!"

Jairus's Daughter _Mark 5:21-43_

As usual, Jesus was surrounded by people who wanted Him to heal their sick or do other miracles for them. Jairus, a leader of one local synagogue, heard that Jesus was nearby and he raced out to see Him. He pushed his way through the crowd and fell at Jesus' feet. "Sir, my little girl is very sick. She is about to die. Please come to my house and heal her," the man begged.

Jesus started to go with the man as the crowd pushed in around Him. A woman who had been sick for 12 years was in the crowd. She had so much faith in Jesus that she believed that if she could just touch the hem of His robe she would be healed. So she reached through the crowd and grabbed His robe. Jesus stopped immediately and asked, "Who touched me?" His disciples couldn't believe He asked that because there were people all around Him. "I felt power go out from me," Jesus said. "Who touched me?"

The woman stepped up and admitted that she did it. "I just wanted to be well because I have been sick for so long," she said.

Jesus was touched by her faith. "Your faith has made you well," He said.

While Jesus was talking to her, Jairus' servant came up and said, "Don't bother Jesus anymore. It's too late. Your daughter is dead." But Jesus ignored this and went on to Jairus's house.

"Don't be afraid. Just trust me," He told Jairus. He only let Peter, James, and John go with Him to Jairus's house. When He arrived there people were crying and sobbing. "Why all this crying?" He asked. "The girl isn't dead. She is just sleeping." The people made fun of Him but He told them all to leave the house. Then He took Jairus, the girl's mother, and His three disciples with Him into the girl's room. He took her hand and said, "Get up, little girl." The girl got up right away and began walking around the room! Her parents were so thankful and amazed. Jesus told them to give the girl something to eat.

Jesus Feeds 5,000

Matthew 14:15-21; Mark 6:35-44; Luke 9:12-17; John 6:1-13

J esus was trying to get some alone time but everywhere He went large crowds of people followed Him. He and His disciples got on a boat to get away from the crowds for a while, but when the boat docked He found that the people had rushed across land and were there waiting for Him. He was filled with love for the people so He healed the sick people

they had brought to Him and He taught them about God. The afternoon passed quickly and when evening came the disciples came to Jesus and said, "Send the people away so they can go into the villages and get food."

But Jesus had another idea. He said, "No, you get food for them."

"That's just not possible," the disciples said. "We don't have enough money to buy food for all these people."

"Do you have any food at all?" Jesus asked.

"There is a young boy in the crowd who has a lunch of five loaves of bread and two fish. He says he will give it to us. But it isn't enough to feed all these people."

"Get the young boy's lunch for me," Jesus said. "Then have all the people sit down in groups of 50." Jesus took the loaves and fish and lifted them up toward Heaven and asked God to bless it. He began breaking the fish and bread into pieces and the disciples passed it out to the people. There were 5,000 men in that crowd. Everyone had all they wanted to eat. When they had finished eating the disciples picked up the leftover food. They collected 12 baskets of leftover food and it all came from five loaves of bread and two fish!

Jesus Walks on Water

Matthew 14:22-33; Mark 6:47-51; John 6:16-21

One time when Jesus had been teaching all day He needed some time alone. So He sent His disciples on to Bethsaida by boat. Meanwhile, He went up into the hills to be alone and pray.

During the night the disciples were in a boat out in the middle of the lake and Jesus was still on the land. They were rowing hard into the wind and the waves were bouncing their little boat all around. At about three o'clock in

the morning Jesus came to His friends, walking on top of the water! He started to walk right past them but when His friends saw Him they screamed because they thought He was a ghost! But Jesus said, "Calm down. It's me. Don't be afraid."

Just then, Peter called to Him, "Lord, if that's really You out there on the water, call to me and I will walk on the water too!"

"OK," Jesus said, "Come on."

Peter jumped out of the boat and began walking on the water toward Jesus. But when he looked around at the big waves surrounding him, he was afraid and he sank into the water. "Save me!" he called to Jesus.

Instantly, Jesus reached out His hand and grabbed Peter. "You don't have much faith," Jesus said to him. "Why did you doubt me?"

Then He climbed into the boat with the disciples and the wind calmed down right away. The disciples were amazed. They were still trying to understand the miracle when He fed the 5,000 people.

The Transfiguration

Matthew 17:1-13; Mark 9:2-13; Luke 9:28-36

Jesus knew that His ministry on Earth was winding down. The end of His life was getting closer and closer. His disciples didn't seem to understand that though. After one particularly hard talk He had with them He took Peter, James, and John with Him up on a high mountain. No one else was with them; just the four of them were alone on the mountain.

Peter, James, and John were amazed

because as they watched, Jesus' appearance changed completely. His face shone as bright as the sun. They could barely look at Him because His face was so bright. His clothing even changed from His normal appearance. He was suddenly wearing robes that were brilliant white! The disciples had never seen anything like it! Suddenly, two more men were there with Jesus. The disciples

recognized them as Moses and Elijah. The two old prophets began to talk with Jesus about how He was going to finish God's plan for Him by dying in Jerusalem. Peter was so completely overwhelmed with the glory of what he saw—two famous old prophets and Jesus glowing brightly. He raced up to Jesus and said, "This is wonderful. It is amazing! If You want, I will build three shrines right now to honor this experience. One will be for You, one for Moses, and one for Elijah."

While Peter was speaking, a cloud came down from Heaven and settled over them. Peter, James, and John were terrified because they couldn't see anything at all through the cloud. They heard a voice coming from Heaven that said, "This is my beloved Son and I am very happy with Him. Listen closely to Him." The disciples fell down on the ground and covered their eyes.

When the cloud lifted, Moses and Elijah were gone. Jesus came over to His friends and told them to get up. "Don't be afraid," He said. "Don't tell anyone what you have seen here until I have risen from the dead."

The disciples were not sure what He meant by that. But they did have a question, "Why do the religious leaders insist that Elijah has to return before the Messiah comes?"

Jesus said, "Elijah is coming first to set everything straight. But the truth is that he already came but no one recognized him. They mistreated him and soon the Son of Man will be mistreated too."

The Last Days

Jesus was sent to Earth by His Father for a specific reason—to make a way for people to be able to connect with God. The end of that plan took Jesus to the cross where He died for the sins of everyone. He tried and tried to tell His disciples that He was going to die but they just never understood. Now the end of His time on Earth was coming. They were going to have to understand quickly.

Jesus Is Anointed *John 12:1-8*

Jesus knew that His ministry on Earth was getting close to being over. He had tried to tell His disciples what was coming, but they didn't ever really understand. One night Jesus and His friends were having dinner at the home of Mary, Martha, and Lazarus. Martha served the dinner and while they were eating, Mary brought in a jar of very expensive perfume. She went right up to Jesus and slowly poured the perfume on his feet then wiped them dry using her own hair. The sweet fragrance of the perfume filled the house. Jesus' disciples watched her do this. Some of them got very upset. Judas Iscariot said, "What a waste of money! This expensive perfume could have been sold for a lot of money and that money could have been used to help the poor!" Judas didn't really care about the poor people. He was in charge of all the disciples' money and he often stole money from their funds for his own use.

Jesus had an answer. "Don't stop her from doing such a good thing for me. Listen, you will always have poor people with you but I will not be here much longer. She has poured this perfume on me to prepare my body for burial. I promise you that whenever my story is told throughout the world, what this woman has done will be mentioned."

Jesus Enters Jerusalem

Matthew 21:1-11; Mark 11:1-11; Luke 19:28-40; John 12:12-50

Jesus and His disciples walked toward Jerusalem. He knew He was heading toward the end of His earthly life. They came to the town of Bethphage and Bethany at the Mount of Olives. They stopped there and Jesus chose two of His followers to go on ahead. "Go into that little town over there," He said. "You will find a donkey tied up there and its young colt beside it. Untie them and bring them to me. If anyone questions what you are

doing just tell them that the Lord needs them and they will let you take them."

Jesus arranged this because the prophets had written that the king of Israel would ride into Jerusalem on a donkey or a donkey's colt.

The two disciples did what Jesus instructed and they came back with the two animals. They threw their own robes on the colt's back and Jesus sat on it to ride into Jerusalem.

As He came down the path, people lined both sides of the street. People took off their robes and cloaks and threw them onto the path ahead of Him so the colt walked on them. Other people ran to cut branches off of the palm trees near the road. They spread the palm branches on the road too. As Jesus rode by, the people shouted, "Praise God for the Son of David! Praise the One who comes in the name of the Lord! Praise God in the highest Heaven!"

The whole city of Jerusalem knew that Jesus had arrived. The religious leaders heard the crowd cheering for Him and they were angry. "Make those people be quiet!" they shouted.

Jesus had an answer, "If the people were quiet, then the stones along the road would burst into cheers!" That comment made the religious leaders even angrier.

The Last Supper

Matthew 26:17-30; Mark 14:12-26; Luke 22:7-20; John 13:1-17

I t was nearly time to celebrate the Passover Feast. Jesus' disciples came to Him and asked, "Where do You want us to go to prepare the Passover meal?"

"Go into the city," Jesus said, "and you will see a man carrying a pitcher of water. Follow him to the house he enters. Go in after him and find the owner of the house. Tell him that the

teacher says that His time has come. Tell him that I wish to eat the Passover meal with my friends at his house. He will lead you to a large upstairs room that is already set up for us. Prepare the supper there." Two of Jesus' disciples went into the city and everything happened just as Jesus said it would. They prepared the meal for everyone else.

Later that evening Jesus and the other disciples arrived. The 12 sat around Him at a table eating the supper. Jesus knew that it was about time for His life on Earth to come to an end. Some very difficult things were going to happen to Him. Judas Iscariot had already made a deal with the religious leaders to turn Jesus over to them. Jesus felt it was urgent now for His followers to understand Him. So He got up from the table where they were all sitting, got a towel and a bowl of water, and began to wash the feet of each disciple. After He washed them He dried them with the towel. When it was Peter's turn, Peter resisted. He said, "Why are You washing my feet?"

"I know that You don't understand why I am doing this right now but you will someday," Jesus said.

"No, I don't want You to wash my feet," Peter said and he pulled his feet away from Jesus.

"If I don't wash you then you are not a part of my family," Jesus answered.

"Then don't just wash my feet, wash my hands and head too!" Peter cried.

"That isn't necessary," Jesus answered. "A person who has washed himself only needs his feet cleaned when coming inside. You are clean, but that isn't true of everyone in this room." Jesus knew that Judas had already agreed to betray Him.

When Jesus finished washing their feet, He said, "Do you understand why I did this? Since I have washed your feet, you should do the same for others. Go out and serve others. You will be blessed if you do this."

The meal continued and as they were talking, Jesus said, "The truth is that one of you sitting here with me will be the one who betrays me."

The disciples were very upset that He would say such a thing and even more upset that one of them would do it. "Is it me?" some asked. "Am I the one?" others questioned.

Jesus said, "It is one of you who is eating with me now. I must die as the Scriptures said long ago. But it will be a terrible thing for the one who betrays me. It would be better for him if he had never been born!"

Jesus picked up a loaf of bread and broke it in half. He asked God to bless it then broke it into pieces and passed it out to His disciples. He said, "Take this and eat it because this is my body."

Then He picked up a cup of wine and thanked God for it. He gave it to them and they passed it around the table and each one took a drink from it. Jesus said, "This is my blood which is poured out for the new agreement between God and His people. I will not drink wine again until the day I drink it in God's kingdom."

Then He led them in singing a hymn before they left that upper room and went out to the Mount of Olives.

Jesus Is Arrested in the Garden

Matthew 26:36-56; Mark 14:32-65: Luke 22:39-53; John 18:1-14

J esus and His closest friends, the disciples, walked up the Mount of Olives and He led them to a garden called Gethsemane. Jesus said, "Sit here while I go and pray." He took Peter, James, and John and they went a little way off from the others.

Jesus knelt down and began to pray and He was filled with agony and great distress. He said, "My very soul is crushed with grief. Stay here with me and watch." Then He walked a few steps away from them and fell face down on the ground. He prayed that, if it was

at all possible, God might change the events that were going to happen that night. "My Dear Father, I know that all things are possible with You. I want You to take away the suffering that is going to happen to me; still I want Your will more than anything, not mine."

Jesus went back to Peter, James, and John and found them sound asleep. He woke them up and said, "Couldn't you stay awake and watch with me for even one hour? Stay alert and pray! If you don't, temptation will overwhelm you because the spirit is willing but the body is weak."

Then Jesus went away from them and prayed again. When He came back they were sleeping again! He woke them and they didn't know what to say to Him. Jesus went away a third time and prayed. He repeated His plea for God to take away the suffering that was coming but He also stated again that He wanted God's will, not His own. He came back to His disciples and once again they were sleeping. "Enough!" He shouted. "It's too late now. The time has come. The one who will betray me is here."

Just then a mob of angry people came up carrying swords and clubs. Judas Iscariot, one of Jesus' disciples, was leading the group. Judas walked right up to Jesus and kissed Him on the cheek. That was a signal the soldiers had arranged with Judas to know which person was Jesus so they could arrest Him. Jesus looked solemnly at Judas and said, "Go ahead and do what you have to do." Some of the soldiers grabbed Jesus and arrested Him. Peter grabbed his sword and cut off one of the ears of a soldier. "Put your sword away," Jesus said. "This is what my Father has for me to do." He touched the side of the soldier's face and his ear was just fine again. Then He said, "Am I some dangerous criminal that you must come with swords and clubs to arrest me? I have been in the temple every day. You could have arrested me there." Jesus' disciples were confused and frightened by these events so they all ran away. Every one of them.

Trial and Denial *Matthew 26:57-75; Mark 14:53-72;*
Luke 22:54-71; John 18:12-27

The soldiers led Jesus to the home of Caiaphas, the high priest. Teachers and religious leaders gathered there for Jesus' immediate trial. Peter followed along behind the crowd. He wanted to know what was happening but didn't want anyone to see him. He went inside and sat with the guards to see what was going to happen. Meanwhile all the powerful

priests and the high council were scurrying around to find witnesses to testify against Jesus. They wanted witnesses to tell lies about Him so they could justify having Him put to death. They found several who were willing to lie, but they couldn't find a testimony that would cause the death penalty. Some of the lies even contradicted each other. Finally, the priests found two men who

said, "We heard this man declare that He could destroy the temple and then rebuild it in three days without using human hands."

The high priest turned to Jesus and said, "What do You have to say for yourself? Are You going to answer these charges?" But Jesus remained silent. The high priest got angry and demanded, "I insist that You tell us whether You are the Messiah, the Son of the living God!"

"I am. You will one day see me sitting at God's right hand in the place of power and coming on the clouds of Heaven," Jesus said.

That was all the high priest needed to hear. He tore his clothes to show how shocked he was. "We don't need any other witnesses," he said to the council. "You heard this blasphemy. What is your verdict?" They all voted to condemn Jesus to death.

Then some of them walked up to Jesus and spit on Him. They put a blindfold on Him and hit Him and shouted, "Hey Prophet, tell us who hit You that time!"

Meanwhile Peter was below in the courtyard of the house. He was warming his hands at the fire when a girl who worked for the high priest noticed him. She stared at him for a few minutes and then said, "I recognize you. You were with Jesus before."

"I was not!" Peter said. "I don't even know what you are talking about!" He left and went away from the girl.

Later he was out by the gate when another girl saw him and said, "This man was with Jesus. I saw him!"

"I don't even know the man!" Peter shouted.

A little later some other people said to him, "You must be one of Jesus' followers because you have a Galilean accent."

"I swear that I do not know Him!" Peter said. Just then he heard a rooster crow. Peter remembered that the previous day when he was saying that he would always stand strong with Him, Jesus had said that Peter would deny Him three times before the rooster crowed. Peter ran away, crying harder than he ever had.

The Road to Golgotha

Matthew 27:11-33; Mark 15:1-22; Luke 23:1-26; John 18:28–19:17

The high priests and the high council condemned Jesus to death but they didn't have the final authority. He had to appear before Pilate, the Roman governor, before the sentence could be carried out. "Are You the King of the Jews?" Pilate asked Jesus.

"Yes, what you say is true," Jesus answered.

Then the room filled with the priests and religious leaders who hated Him. They shouted accusations at Him. But Jesus didn't respond to any of their accusations. He remained completely quiet.

"Don't You hear what they are saying?" Pilate asked. "Don't You have any response to their accusations?" But Jesus didn't say a word.

It was the custom during the Passover celebration for the governor to release one prisoner whom the people chose to set free. They could choose any one they wanted. There was one famous prisoner that year named Barabbas. As the crowd around Pilate grew larger and larger, he asked them, "Which prisoner do you want me to release for you this year? Do you want Barabbas or Jesus?" Pilate knew that the religious leaders had condemned Jesus only because they

were jealous of His popularity and he thought the people might set Him free. But the religious leaders and priests had planted the idea with the crowd to ask for Barabbas to be set free and for Jesus to be killed. So when the governor asked which prisoner they wanted freed the crowd shouted, "Barabbas!"

"But if I free Barabbas then what should I do with Jesus?" Pilate asked.

"Crucify Him!" the crowd shouted.

"Why, what has He done?" Pilate asked.

"Crucify Him! Crucify Him! Crucify Him!" the shouts grew louder and louder!

Pilate saw that the situation was hopeless so he called for a servant to bring him a bowl of water. Right in front of the crowd, he washed his hands and said, "I am innocent of this man's blood. Responsibility for His death is on your heads."

The people shouted, "We'll take it. Crucify Him!"

So Pilate released Barabbas and ordered that Jesus be beaten with a whip that had metal tied in the ends of it.

Then he turned Him over to the soldiers to be crucified.

The soldiers stripped off Jesus' clothes and put a red robe on Him. They made a crown out of thorny vines and put it on His head and they made Him hold a stick in His hand like a scepter. Then they bowed down in front of Him and said, "Hail, king of the Jews!" But they were just making fun of Him. They spit on Him and grabbed the stick out of His hand and beat Him with it. Finally they grew tired of doing this so they put His own clothes back on Him and led Him out of the building to be crucified.

They made Jesus carry the heavy crossbeam that would be a part of the cross on which He would die. He was weak because of the beatings and He fell down under the weight of the cross. One of the soldiers grabbed a man from the crowd named Simon, and they made him carry Jesus' cross to the hill called Golgotha where the crucifixion would take place.

Jesus Dies on the Cross

Matthew 27:32-61; Mark 14:21-47; Luke 23:26-56; John 19:16-42

About nine o'clock in morning the soldiers led Jesus to Golgotha where He was nailed to the cross. His cross was centered between the crosses of two thieves who were also being crucified that day. Before they put Jesus on the cross the soldiers offered Him some wine (drugged with myrrh which would have numbed His senses) but He refused it. They took off His clothes and threw dice to see which one of them would get to keep His robe. A sign was hung at the top of His cross that said, "This is Jesus, king of the Jews." People who came to watch

Him be killed shouted, "He saved other people, let Him save himself!" and "Go ahead king of the Jews, save yourself!" The soldiers offered Him drinks of sour wine and made fun of Him.

The criminal on one side Him said, "You say You are the Messiah? OK, prove it by saving yourself and us too!"

But the criminal on the other side stopped those comments by saying, "Don't you even fear God when you are dying? You and I deserve to die for the bad things we have done. But this man has done nothing wrong." Then he turned to Jesus and said, "Jesus, remember me when You come to rule."

Jesus said, "You will be with me this day in Heaven!"

Jesus' mother was there with some other women watching all that was happening. Jesus saw her standing near one of His disciples whom He loved very much. He looked at His mother and said, "Woman, he is your son." Then He turned to His disciple and said, "She is your mother now."

By this time it was about noon. Even so, the sky grew very dark and the whole land stayed dark until 3:00 in the afternoon. Jesus called out, "My God, My God, why have You forsaken me?"

Then He shouted, "Father, into Your hands I put my Spirit!" Then He died. Suddenly, the thick veil that hung in the temple was torn apart from top to bottom. The earth shook like an earthquake, rocks split apart, and graves broke open.

When the captain of the guards who was in charge of the crucifixions saw what had happened, he said, "Surely this man was God's Son." All of Jesus' friends who were watching the crucifixion went home with hearts filled with sadness.

The Jewish leaders didn't want the bodies hanging on the crosses the next day because it was the Sabbath so they asked Pilate to hurry up their deaths by breaking their legs. The soldiers came to break the legs of the two criminals, but seeing that Jesus was already dead, they didn't break His legs. However one of the soldiers stuck his spear into Jesus' side and blood and water flowed out.

A man named Joseph from Arimathea asked if he could have Jesus' body to bury Him. He had a brand new tomb that no

one had been buried in yet. He was given permission to take Jesus' body down and other people brought ointments and perfumes to put on the body. That was the Jewish custom before burial. They wrapped Jesus in special strips of cloth for burial and they laid Him in the tomb that was like a large cave. A heavy stone was rolled in front of the opening of the tomb. Mary Magdalene and the other woman named Mary stayed nearby and saw all of this happen.

Jesus Is Alive!

Matthew 28:1-10; Mark 16:1-11; Luke 24:1-12; John 20:1-18

Early on Sunday morning Mary Magdalene and some of the other women came to the tomb where Jesus had been buried. They hadn't been able to properly prepare Jesus' body for burial because of the Sabbath and now that it was over they could put perfumes and oils on Him. As they left town and began walking to the tomb, one of the women wondered how they were going to move the heavy stone away from the opening of the tomb. They were amazed when they got close to the tomb to see that the stone had already been moved! The tomb was open! The women rushed into the tomb only

to find that Jesus' body wasn't there! The women were confused about what could have happened to Him. Suddenly two men appeared. They were dressed in brilliant white robes. The women were terrified but the two men, who were angels, said, "Why are you looking in a tomb for someone who is alive? The one you are looking for isn't here. He has risen from the dead! Don't you remember that He told you He would be crucified and come back to life on the third day?"

Then the women remembered that Jesus had said that.

Mary Magdalene was standing outside the tomb trying to understand what had happened. She was crying when she saw a man standing nearby. He asked her why she was crying. Mary thought he must be the caretaker of the garden so she asked him, "Sir, tell me where you have taken His body and I will go get Him."

"Mary," the man gently said. That's when she realized that it was Jesus!

The women rushed back to town to tell Jesus' disciples that He was alive. Peter and the other disciples ran to the tomb as fast as they could to see if it was true. Peter ran into the tomb and found the strips of cloths that had been wrapped around Jesus' body lying neatly folded. He wasn't there. He was alive!

The Road to Emmaus *Luke 24:13-35*

That very same day two of Jesus' followers were walking to the village of Emmaus. They were talking about everything that had happened the last couple of days. Suddenly Jesus was walking along with them but they didn't recognize Him because God didn't let them. They didn't even know where He had come from.

"You are having a serious conversation," Jesus said to them. "What are you so upset about?"

They stopped and looked at Him with sadness in their faces. Then one of them said, "You must be the only person in all of Jerusalem who hasn't heard what has happened here in the last few days."

"What things are you talking about?" Jesus asked.

"Jesus of Nazareth was crucified," they said. "He was a prophet who did amazing miracles. He taught about God and the people respected Him. But our leading priests and religious leaders arrested Him and had Him condemned to death. We thought He was the Messiah. This all happened three days ago. Some of the women of our group went to His tomb early this morning. They came back with the incredible report that He has risen from the dead. They saw angels who said He is alive! Some of the

men of our group ran to the tomb and sure enough the body was gone."

Then Jesus said, "You foolish people. You find it so hard to believe what the prophets wrote in Scripture. Didn't the prophets say that the Messiah would have to suffer terrible things before returning to Heaven?" Jesus quoted passages from the Old Testament to back up what He was saying.

By this time they were very near Emmaus and it was quite late. The two men asked Jesus to come in and stay overnight. He went in with them and they prepared a meal. When Jesus sat down to eat He took a loaf of bread and asked God to bless it, then He broke it and gave it to them. At that very moment, God opened their eyes and gave them understanding so they knew it was Jesus sitting there with them! Just as they recognized Him, He disappeared!

"We knew He was someone special as He talked with us," the men said to each other. They hurried back to Jerusalem to tell Jesus' other followers that they had seen Him.

Jesus Appears to the Disciples

Mark 16:14-20; Luke 24:33-49; John 20:19-31

Jesus' disciples were frightened by all that had happened. The day that Jesus' tomb was discovered empty, His followers were together in the same room with the door locked. They sat in sad stillness just whispering their confusion and grief.

Suddenly, Jesus was standing there in the room with them! They were terrified. They thought it was a ghost standing there. "Peace be with you," Jesus said to them. He held out His hands so they could see where the nails had been and He showed them the hole in

His side where the soldier had stabbed Him. Then the disciples knew that this man standing before them really was Jesus and they were filled with joy!

Jesus looked around the room at His friends and said, "Do you have anything to eat?" They gave Him a piece of fish and He ate it. Then He said, "The prophets wrote a long time ago that the Messiah must suffer and die and rise from the dead. I'm giving you the authority to take this message of repentance to the whole world. Tell everyone that there is forgiveness of sins for all who follow me. You are to testify of that. And soon I will give you the Holy Spirit, which My Father promised to you."

One of the disciples, Thomas, was not with his friends when Jesus appeared to them. The others told Thomas that they had seen Jesus. Their excitement should have been catching, but Thomas didn't believe them. He didn't believe Jesus was alive. He said, "I won't believe it until I see the nail prints in His hands and touch His side."

Eight days later the disciples were in the locked room again and Thomas was with them. Suddenly Jesus was there with them again. "See my hands, Thomas. Touch my side. Believe that I am here with you."

"My Lord and my God," Thomas said. He was convinced.

"You believe because you have seen me," Jesus said. "How very blessed are those who believe without seeing me."

Breakfast with Jesus *John 21:1-14*

here were many times that Jesus appeared to people after He was resurrected. One day many of Jesus' disciples were near the Sea of Tiberias. Peter, who was a fisherman before Jesus called him to be His follower, said, "I'm going fishing." Everyone decided to go with him. So they all went out in the boat and they fished all night without catching even one fish.

About dawn they came back to shore and saw a man standing on the beach. It was Jesus, but they were kept from recognizing Him. He called out to them, "My friends, have you caught any fish?"

They told Him that they hadn't.

"Well, throw your nets out on the right side of the boat and you will catch plenty of fish," He said. They did what He said and caught so many fish that they couldn't pull in the net.

Suddenly, John, the disciple who was called the one Jesus loved, recognized the man on the beach. "It is Jesus!" he cried. When Peter heard that he jumped into the water and hurried to the shore. The others stayed in the boat and brought it and all the fish to the shore. When they got to the beach they saw a small fire burning and fish frying over it. There was bread for them too. "Bring me some of the fish you caught," Jesus said. Simon went into the boat and brought out over 100 large fish. It was amazing that the net hadn't torn with that many fish in it. Jesus finished cooking the food then invited the disciples to come have breakfast with Him.

Peter Is Restored   *John 21:15-17*

Peter had failed. He thought His faith in Jesus was really strong. But when Jesus was being tried before the high council, Peter denied even knowing Jesus. He didn't just do this once or twice; he denied knowing Jesus three times! He must have felt that Jesus was very disappointed in him.

After Jesus came back to life He and Peter had a conversation. Jesus asked, "Peter, do you love me?"

"Yes, Lord," Peter answered, "You know that I do."

"Then feed my lambs," Jesus said.

"Peter, do you love me?" Jesus asked again.

"Yes, Lord," Peter answered, "You know that I love You."

"Then take care of my sheep," Jesus said.

"Peter, do you love me?" Jesus asked a third time.

Peter was sad that Jesus had asked him the same question three times in a row. He said, "Jesus, You know everything. You know that I do love You!"

"Then feed my sheep," Jesus said.

Jesus Goes Home

Mark 16:19, 20; Luke 24:50-53; Acts 1:6-11

The disciples were thrilled that Jesus was alive again. They had hope for the future because He was alive again. They kept asking Jesus questions about when He was going to free Israel and set up His kingdom. They didn't really understand what Jesus had been teaching them.

"My Father sets all the plans for His kingdom. I don't even know His plans," Jesus told them. "When the Holy Spirit comes you will receive amazing power," Jesus told them. "You will tell people about me and my work and my teachings. You will tell people right here in Jerusalem, in Judea, in Samaria, and in the whole world!"

Not long after telling them these things, Jesus was taken up into the sky while they watched. He disappeared into a cloud and the disciples strained their eyes trying to see where He had gone. While they were still looking, two men in white robes were suddenly standing there with them. "What are you looking for?" the men in white asked. "Jesus isn't here. He has been taken away and has gone to Heaven. Someday He will come back in just the same way as He left!"

THE YOUNG CHURCH

Just before Jesus went back to Heaven He promised that the Holy Spirit would come to give power and strength to the believers. Then it was up to them to join together and keep spreading the message of God's love to the rest of the world. That's how the young church was born. The believers joined together for strength and to work together as God's people in the world. However, it wasn't always easy for them.

Pentecost *Acts 2:1-42*

S even weeks after Jesus came back to life, all the believers in Jerusalem were together in one place. Suddenly they heard a sound like a strong, roaring wind. The strange thing was that the sound was inside the room! It sounded like a powerful storm—inside! Then, something that looked like little flames of fire appeared in the room. The flames floated around the room and one

flame settled on each person in the room. That was the Holy Spirit! Jesus had promised that God would send Him. Each person in the room was filled with the Holy Spirit and each person immediately began speaking in another language than his own. The Holy Spirit gave them that ability!

There were some people in Jerusalem who were from other countries. They heard all the commotion so they came to see what was going on. These

people were amazed to hear their own languages being spoken by people who were from Galilee. "How is this happening?" they asked each other. "These people are all from Galilee but they are speaking the languages of Asia, Egypt, Cyrene, and Rome. We are hearing them speak wonderful things about God and we can understand it!" They were all amazed but there were some in the crowd who just thought that the believers were drunk.

Peter stepped up and the other disciples stood with him. "Listen, none of us is drunk. We haven't been drinking at all. No, what you are seeing here is what was predicted years ago by the prophet Joel. He said: 'God says that in the last days I will pour out my spirit on the people. They will prophesy. I will cause wonders in the heavens. And anyone who calls on my name will be saved.' Listen to me! God told you that Jesus of Nazareth is His Son. He did miracles and signs but you people crucified Him. God raised Him from the dead and we all know it is true. Now He is back in Heaven with His Father and He has given us His Holy Spirit. That's why we have the power to speak in these languages."

The people were amazed at what Peter said. "What do we do now?" they asked.

"Stop sinning. Turn away from sin and follow God. Be baptized in the name of Jesus and accept forgiveness of your sins. Then you will receive the Holy Spirit also." Peter preached for a long time. Many people believed what Peter said and about 3,000 people were baptized and added to the young church that day.

Helping One Another

Acts 2:42-47; 4:32-37

Right after God sent the Holy Spirit to the believers, some wonderful things began to happen. The believers were amazed at the power they had because of the Holy Spirit. They were filled with great love for one another and they cared very much about each other. This care and concern was from God. The believers met together constantly, enjoying each other's company and

helping each other with whatever needs there were. There was not selfishness among them. They shared everything they had—food, clothing, and money. Some people even sold land they owned, their houses, or other possessions and shared the money they got with others in the young church. Because of their generosity and care, no one was actually poor.

The believers worshiped together at the temple every day, not just once a week. They met often in each other's homes and shared the Lord's Supper and regular meals too. They loved being together and praising God. Every single day God added more people to their group. The church was growing very fast!

Peter and John Heal a Lame Man

Acts 3:1-10

Peter and John went to the Temple each day to participate in the afternoon prayer service. One day they went to the temple as usual but as they got near it they saw a man being carried in. He had been unable to walk his whole life. Each day he was carried in and put down by the gate so he could beg for money from the people who went into the temple. The

man saw Peter and John as they walked toward the temple and he called out to them to ask them for some money.

Peter and John stopped and looked at the man. "Look at us," Peter said. The man gladly looked at them because he expected them to give him some money. Peter said, "I don't have any money to give to you. But I will give you what I do have. In the name of Jesus Christ, get up and walk."

Peter took the man's hand and helped him get up. Instantly the man's legs and feet straightened out and became strong. He stood up for the first time in his life and he began to walk! All the people standing around were amazed. They saw the man walking around and praising God and they knew he was the man who had never walked before. They were in awe of the wonderful thing that had happened to the man.

Stephen Is Stoned *Acts 6:6–7:60*

Stephen was one of the strong believers in the young church. The Holy Spirit filled him with God's power, love, and grace and helped him do amazing miracles. But one day some men from other cities got into a debate with Stephen. None of them were able to match Stephen's wisdom because his came from the Holy Spirit. That made the men angry so they convinced some other people to tell lies about Stephen so he would be arrested. They lied that they had heard him say bad things about Moses and even God. Of course the religious leaders were very upset by these accusations. So they had Stephen arrested and brought before the high council for trial. The same witnesses told more lies. "We've heard him say that Jesus is going to destroy the temple and change all the customs that Moses taught us."

Just then every person in the council turned and stared at Stephen because his face began to glow as bright as the sun. Then the high priest asked Stephen if the accusations were true. Stephen replied, "Brothers, remember that God appeared to our father Abraham and told him to leave his home and move to the land God showed him. Abraham obeyed and God promised to give him this land and many, many ancestors. God gave him the son Isaac, and Isaac's son Jacob became the father of the 12 tribes of Israel. Remember how 11 of these sons were jealous of their brother Joseph and they sold him into slavery. But God allowed Joseph to save the nation of Egypt and even his own family from a famine. You recall how our people became slaves in Egypt and then Moses was born and God sent him to lead the people to freedom. God gave Moses the laws and commandments by which we live. Moses told the people that God would raise up a prophet. The people turned against Moses and had Aaron make them a golden calf to worship. Then God turned away from the people. Years later Joshua led the people and then there were the years of King David, a man who found favor with God. David's son, Solomon, built God's temple.

"You stubborn people. You know our people's history with God. Yet your ancestors persecuted the prophets. You killed Jesus, God's own Son!"

The religious leaders were very angry at the things Stephen said to them. They shook their fists at him and shouted at him. But God gave Stephen a vision of the heavens opening and Jesus standing before him. He wasn't afraid of anything they said to him. So they dragged Stephen outside of the city and threw stones at him until he was dead. As he was dying Stephen prayed for the people who were killing him. He said, "Lord, don't charge them with this sin." Then he died.

Philip and the Ethiopian *Acts 8:26-40*

od had a special job for Philip. An angel of God came to Philip and told him to go down a certain road—the road that went from Jerusalem to Gaza. Philip didn't know why he was told to do this, but he obeyed. As he was walking down the road he saw a carriage driving by. There was a man in the carriage who was very important in the court of the queen of Ethiopia. He

had gone to Jerusalem to worship in the temple and was on his way home now. He was sitting in the carriage reading from the book of Isaiah.

The Holy Spirit said to Philip, "Go over to the carriage and walk along beside it." Philip immediately obeyed and he heard the man reading aloud the words of Isaiah.

"Do you understand what you're reading?" Philip asked the man.

"No, how could I?" the man

answered. "There is no one here to explain it to me." Then the man begged Philip to come into the carriage and explain what the words meant. This is what he was reading about:

"He was led like a sheep to the slaughter. And just like a lamb before his killers, he did not open his mouth. He was humiliated and no justice was given to him. What can be said about his descendants? His life was taken from this earth."

"Who is the prophet Isaiah talking about?" the man asked Philip.

Philip explained this Scripture and used several others to share the good news of Jesus Christ with the man. The man understood and wanted to be baptized right away. He ordered the carriage driver to stop and went over to a nearby lake. Philip baptized the man right there on the road. When the man was lifted out of the water, God took Philip away and the man never saw him again. But he went on his way praising God and celebrating his new life!

Saul Is Changed! *Acts 9:1-19*

S aul was a famous man but not for doing something good. He was famous for punishing the people who believed that Jesus was the Messiah. He tried to put them in pris-

on. He threatened them. He tried to hurt them. Saul thought he was right in doing this. He even thought God was pleased with him because Saul believed that Jesus was a fake. Saul had pretty

much taken care of all the believers in the area where he lived and he wanted to go to Damascus to stop the believers there from talking about Jesus. He got letters from the high priest to the synagogues in Damascus that supported what he wanted to do. He planned to round up all the believers in Damascus and bring them back to Jerusalem in chains.

Saul was on the road to Damascus and was traveling with a group of people. Suddenly a bright light shined down directly on Saul. He was so shocked that he fell to the ground. Then a loud voice said, "Saul, Saul, why are you persecuting me?"

"Who is speaking to me?" Saul asked.

"I am Jesus," the voice said. "It is me you are persecuting. Now, I want you to get up and to into the city. I will tell you what to do next."

The men who were traveling with Saul were speechless. They could hear the voice but they couldn't see the man who was speaking. Saul tried to get up and that's when he realized that he was blind! He couldn't see at all! So the men with Saul had to lead him into the city. He stayed there in Damascus for three days without being able to see a thing. For those three days Saul had no food or water.

There was a follower of Jesus in Damascus named Ananias. He had a vision that God told him to go talk to Saul.

God told Ananias that Saul was praying right at that moment and God told Saul that a man named Ananias was going to visit him. God said that Ananias would lay hands on Saul and heal his sight. Ananias wasn't too happy about God's instructions. He said, "Lord, I've heard about the terrible things that this man does to Your followers in Jerusalem. We've heard that he is coming here to do the same to us. Do You really want me to go see him?"

"It's OK," God said. "Go ahead and do what I tell you. I have chosen Saul to take my message to the Gentiles as well as the to people of Israel."

So Ananias obeyed God and went to see Saul. He put his hands on Saul's eyes and said, "Brother Saul, God has sent me to you so that you may get your sight back and be filled with God's Holy Spirit." Immediately something that looked like scales fell off Saul's eyes and he could see. Saul was baptized right away and he ate some food and drank some water and got his strength back.

Saul's Escape *Acts 9:20-31*

S aul stayed with some of the believers for a few days and he immediately began preaching in the synagogues that Jesus was truly God's Son. Everyone who heard him was amazed because they knew that only a few days before he was persecuting believers—and now he was one!

The more Saul preached, the more powerful his preaching became. None

of the Jews in Damascus could find fault with him but they were not happy with him. Some of the Jewish leaders got so upset with Saul that they decided to kill him. They were constantly watch-ing for a time they could ambush him. Saul heard about their plans and some of his new friends helped him escape. They had to be sneaky, though, so dur-ing the night they had Saul climb into a

big basket. Then they tied ropes on it and lowered him over the city wall.

Saul went to Jerusalem and tried to meet with the believers there. But they were all afraid of him because they didn't know he had changed. They thought he was pretending to be a believer just to trick them. Barnabas came with him to talk to the believers. He told them how Saul had met the Lord on the way to Damascus and how he preached so powerfully afterwards. So the believers accepted Saul and after that he preached in Jerusalem. His preaching was powerful and it angered the Jewish leaders wherever he went. The young church grew stronger in numbers and in strength because the believers walked with the Lord and were filled with the power of the Holy Spirit.

Dorcas Is Alive! *Acts 9:36-43*

Jesus' followers were sometimes given special abilities through the power of the Holy Spirit. That happened to Peter several times. One time he was called to a town named Joppa. There was a woman in that town named Dorcas who was always showing great kindness to others. Dorcas was especially helpful to the poor. Everyone loved Dorcas for her kind spirit and helpful attitude. Dorcas got sick and her friends rallied around her, doing everything they could think of to make her comfortable and to

help her get well. But nothing they did helped and Dorcas died. Her friends were heartbroken that she was gone. They put special oils and perfumes on her body which was always done before a body was buried. They put her body in an upstairs room and prepared for her funeral. Then they heard that Jesus' follower, Peter, was in a neighboring town. So they sent two men to talk to Peter and beg him to come to Joppa as quickly as possible.

Peter went back to Joppa with the two men and Dorcas's friends took him to the room where her body was lying. The room was filled with her friends, widows, and poor people who were crying. They showed Peter the coats and other pieces of clothing that Dorcas had sewed for them. Pretty much everyone had something that Dorcas had made. Peter asked all the people to leave the room. Then he knelt down beside Dorcas and prayed. After that he turned to her and said, "Get up!" She opened her eyes and when she saw Peter she sat up. He took her hand and helped her stand up. Then Peter called all of Dorcas's friends back into the room and showed them that she was alive.

The news of what happened to Dorcas spread quickly through the whole town and many people believed in Jesus because of it.

Peter and Cornelius *Acts 10*

There was a Roman army officer named Cornelius who lived in the town of Caesarea. Cornelius and his whole household loved and respected God. He gave money to charity and he prayed to God often. One afternoon Cornelius had a vision in which he saw an angel of God standing in front of him calling his name.

"What do you want, sir?" Cornelius asked. He was terrified.

The angel said, "God has heard your prayers for the poor and needy. Now He wants you to send some men down to Joppa to find a man named Peter. They will find him at the home of a man named Simon who lives near the seashore. Ask Peter to come and visit with you." As soon as the angel left, Cornelius called two of his servants and a soldier and sent them to Joppa to find Peter.

The next day, just as Cornelius's servants were about to reach Joppa, Peter had a vision too. He went up on the rooftop of the house to pray. It was about noontime and he was hungry when this happened. He saw the sky open up and a large piece of material was lowered down by the four corners. Inside the fabric were all kinds of animals, reptiles, and birds. Then a voice said, "Peter, get up, kill these animals and eat them."

"No," said Peter. "I have never eaten anything that is unclean and these animals are forbidden by our Jewish laws."

The voice said, "Peter, if God says something is OK, then do not disagree with Him." Peter had this same vision three times before the piece of material disappeared.

Peter was confused. He couldn't figure out what this vision meant. Right at that moment the men from Cornelius's house arrived. They asked to speak to Peter. The Holy Spirit spoke to Peter and told him that some men had arrived to ask him to go with them. The Spirit said that he should go. "All is well," the Holy Spirit said, "because I have sent them to you."

So the men explained why they had come. They told Peter that even though Cornelius was Roman, he honored and obeyed God. They said that an angel told Cornelius to send for Peter. Peter agreed to go with them to visit Cornelius.

Cornelius was waiting for Peter to arrive. He had called all of his relatives and friends to be there to meet Peter. When Peter came into the room, Cornelius fell to the floor in worship. "Get up," Peter said. "I'm just a man like you are." So Cornelius got up and the two

of them talked for a while.

"You know, it is against Jewish laws for me to come into the home of a Gentile," Peter said. "However, God showed me that I should never think of any person as unclean. So I came to see you as soon as you asked. Now, tell me why you sent for me."

Cornelius told Peter about the vision he had when the angel spoke to him. Then Peter knew that his own vision was teaching him that God does not show partiality. God accepts all those who fear and obey Him. Then Peter told all the people in Cornelius's house that God offers peace through Jesus Christ. He told all about Jesus' life, death, and resurrection and even of His appearances after coming back to life. Peter told them that Jesus had given His followers the job of preaching the good news everywhere.

The Holy Spirit helped everyone in Cornelius's house understand what Peter was saying and all of them believed. Some of the Jewish people who had come with Peter were amazed that the Holy Spirit was given to the Gentiles. "Does anyone here object to these new believers being baptized?" Peter asked. No one did object, so Peter gave orders for all of them to be baptized.

Peter Escapes from Prison! *Acts 12:1-19*

A while after Saul's conversion, King Herod Agrippa picked up where Saul had left off and began to persecute the believers. He had James killed and when he saw how happy that made the religious leaders he had Peter arrested to please them. Peter was put in prison guarded by four squads of guards. Each squad had four soldiers in it so 16 guards were assigned to Peter. Herod planned to bring Peter to trial after the Passover celebration. But as soon as they heard that Peter was in prison, the believers began praying earnestly for his protection and freedom.

The night before Peter's trial was supposed to happen, Peter was asleep, chained between two guards. And there were other guards standing at the gates of the prison. Suddenly a bright light filled the cell and an angel stood near

Peter. The angel woke Peter and said, "Get up! You need to get out of here quickly!" Then the chains that were holding Peter to the guards fell off! "Get dressed. Put on your coat and your shoes!" the angel said. The angel led Peter out of the cell. All this time, Peter thought he was dreaming. They walked through the prison, past the first and second guards, and to the big gate of the prison. The gate swung open all by itself and they walked right out. No guards stopped them or asked them any questions. They started walking down the street when the angel suddenly disappeared.

Peter finally realized that God had set him free from prison. He hurried to the house where he knew the other believers were praying for him. He knocked at the door and a servant girl named Rhoda came to see who was there. She recognized Peter's voice and was so excited that she forgot to open the door. Instead Rhoda raced back into the room to tell everyone that Peter was outside. "Peter is at the door! It's Peter!" she cried.

"You're crazy," the other people said. "It must mean that he is dead and his angel is here." Meanwhile Peter kept knocking and calling for them to open the door. Finally someone let him inside. Peter told the believers how God had sent an angel to set him free and lead him out of the prison.

The next morning there was a great problem at the prison when they discovered that Peter was missing. Herod questioned the guards who had been watching Peter and then sentenced them to death.

Preaching God's Word *Acts 13–16*

The believers of the young church took Jesus' command to spread the message of His love seriously. They commissioned Saul and Barnabas to go out from their church and preach the gospel to people who had not heard. God changed Saul's name to Paul and the first missionary trip took Paul and Barnabas to a town called Seleucia and to the island of Cyprus. They

traveled from town to town, preaching and meeting with people. Some people fought them and tried to stop them, but God's power filled them and they could not be stopped. Paul went into the synagogues and talked with the people about the history of how God had worked for His people. He taught them about Jesus' death and resurrection and how He did that for them. Paul taught both the Jews and the Gentiles (people who were not Jewish) about God. The more Paul and Barnabas preached, the angrier the Jewish leaders got. Even so, many people believed the gospel and put their faith in Jesus.

Some of the Jewish leaders got so angry that they decided to attack and stone Paul and Barnabas. But Paul and Barnabas ran for their lives and went to a new city where they continued preaching about Jesus.

They were preaching in Lystra when they saw a man who had been unable to walk since birth. Paul told him to stand up and the man jumped to his feet! The people who were there saw what happened and began shouting that Paul and Barnabas were gods! That made Paul sad. "Don't you understand? We're just people like you, except we are God's servants who are doing His work." They continued traveling and doing God's work until they had a disagreement about taking a young boy named John Mark with them. Paul didn't want him to come so Barnabas and John Mark went on their own trip.

On Paul's second missionary journey he took Silas with him to Derbe and then to Lystra. They met a young boy there named Timothy who was a strong believer and he joined them for part of the trip. One night Paul had a vision while he was sleeping. He saw a man from Macedonia, a place in northern Greece, begging him to come there. "Come and help us!" the man cried. So Paul and Silas left immediately for Macedonia to preach the good news of God's love there.

Lydia Believes *Acts 16:11-15*

One of the stops on Paul's second missionary journey came after he sailed to the island of Samothrace and docked at a city called Neapolis. Then he traveled by land to the city of Philippi, a city in Macedonia. He stayed there several days.

Paul and his friends heard about a group of people who usually met near the river to worship and pray.

On the Sabbath day, the day of worship, they went out to the river to look for the believers. They found a group of women who had gathered to worship there and they sat down to talk with them. One of the women was a businesswoman named Lydia. She was very wealthy because she sold expensive purple cloth in her hometown of Thyatira. Lydia already worshiped God but she listened to Paul explain about Jesus' teachings and His life, death, and resurrection. Lydia believed everything Paul told her and she was baptized that day right there in the river! Several members of her household, servants, and family members, were baptized too. After that she invited Paul and his friends to come and stay at her home as long as they wanted. She kept asking them to come until they finally agreed.

Prison Music *Acts 16:16-40*

One day Paul and Silas saw a girl who had an evil spirit living inside of her body. She was a fortune teller and the people who owned her earned a lot of money from her fortunes. When she saw Paul and Silas, she started shouting, "These men are servants of God and they have come here to tell you how to be saved!"

She did this day after day until Paul finally got tired of it and spoke to the evil spirit living in her, "I command you

to come out of this girl in the name of Jesus Christ!" Instantly the spirit left the girl. However her owners were not happy with Paul because the girl could not earn money for them anymore. They said bad things about Paul and Silas and got the crowd stirred up against them. A mob gathered around them and the officials in the city ordered them stripped naked and beaten with wooden rods. Then they were thrown in prison and the jailer was ordered to make sure they didn't escape. He took them into the deepest, darkest part of the prison and locked their feet in stocks.

At around midnight, Paul and Silas were praying and singing hymns to God's glory. All the other prisoners were listening to them. Suddenly there was a powerful earthquake and the prison doors broke open and the chains holding every prisoner fell off. The jailer woke up when he felt the earthquake and rushed in to find the prison doors open. He thought the prisoners had all escaped so he took out his sword to kill himself. "Wait! Don't hurt yourself!"

Paul shouted. "We're all here! Every prisoner is still here!"

The jailer was shaking with fear but he called for lights and ran to the cell where Paul was. He fell down on his knees and cried, "What must I do to be saved?"

"Believe on the Lord Jesus Christ and you will be saved," Paul said. They explained the whole gospel message to him and that night the jailer and his entire family trusted Jesus. They were baptized immediately. Then the jailer brought Paul and Silas to his home and gave them food.

The next morning the city official sent word to the jailer that he should free Paul and Silas. "You are free to go," he told them.

But Paul said, "Wait a minute. They publicly beat us and put us in jail and we are citizens of Rome. Now they want us to leave quietly? No, we want them to come in person and tell us we can go." The city officials were frightened to hear that Paul and Silas were Roman citizens. They came to the jail and apologized to them and begged them to leave the city.

Paul Preaches in Thessalonica, Berea, and Athens *Acts 17*

Paul and Silas arrived in Thessalonica and as usual Paul went to the synagogue and began teaching about Jesus. He told the people there that Jesus was the Messiah they had been waiting for. He told them how Jesus had died but then was brought back to life. Many of the people there believed what Paul taught and became followers of Jesus. Both men and women believed.

But the Jewish leaders didn't like what Paul was teaching. They were jealous that some of their people were becoming believers. So they found some men out on the street and stirred them up until they formed a mob of angry men who wanted to hurt Paul. The mob attacked the home of Jason because they thought Paul and Silas were there. They didn't find them but they dragged Jason out onto the street and to the city council. "Paul is turning our city upside down with his crazy teachings," they said. "And this man lets them stay in his home. He is guilty of treason against Caesar because they are loyal to the king they call Jesus!" The people in the city and even the officials of the city were thrown into turmoil by these accusations. Finally they let Jason go after he paid a fine.

The believers sent Paul and Silas away to escape the danger. They arrived in Berea and as usual went to the synagogue. The people in Berea were more accepting and listened to Paul's teachings with interest. They read through the Scriptures every day to make sure he was teaching the truth. Many Jews and important Greek women and men believed in Jesus because of Paul and Silas's teachings. But the Jews from Thessalonica heard what was happening and they came to Berea to cause more trouble. The believers in Berea immediately sent Paul on to Athens. Silas and Timothy stayed behind.

When Paul got to Athens he saw idols everywhere in the city. He was very upset by this. He went to the synagogue and spoke every day in the city's public square. He also debated some of the philosophers and told everyone about Jesus' resurrection. They thought he was a little crazy or that he was pushing some strange religion.

The philosophers took Paul to the Council of Philosophers where he was asked to explain more about the strange religion he was teaching. "We have never heard these things you're teaching and we want to know what it is all about," they said. The people in Athens were known for their curiosity and interest in the latest and newest ideas.

Paul stood up before the council and said, "Men of Athens, I can see that you are very religious. I know this because of all the altars and idols I see. One that I saw has an inscription that says, 'To an Unknown God.' You've been worshiping this God without even knowing his name? Well, let me tell you about Him. He is the God who created the world and everything in it. He is Lord of Heaven and Earth and He does not live in some man-made building. He gives life and breath to everything. He wants all nations to seek Him and find Him. Yes, He is not far away from any of us. We should not think of God as an idol made by a stone carver or metal worker. He has forgiven our ignorance about these things in the past but now He commands that everyone turn away from idols and turn to Him. I tell you that He has set a day for judging the world by the man He appointed. He proved who this man is by raising Him from the dead."

When the philosophers heard Paul speaking about Jesus' resurrection some of them laughed at him. But others wanted to hear more about it. Some of them talked with Paul later and became believers as they understood what he taught about Jesus.

Priscilla and Aquila *Acts 18*

When Paul left Athens he went to Corinth. Shortly after arriving there he met a man named Aquila and his wife Priscilla. They were tentmakers who had been sent out of Italy because they were Jews. Paul had been a tentmaker too, so they had that in common. Every Sabbath day Paul went to the synagogue and taught both the Jews and Greeks about Jesus. "Jesus is the Messiah you are looking for," he taught. When the Jewish people argued

with him and even insulted him, Paul said, "You have to live with your choices. I'm going to teach the Gentiles," and he left. Many Gentiles in Corinth heard Paul teach and believed in Jesus because of his message.

One night God spoke to Paul in a dream and told him, "Don't be afraid. Speak out with courage. I am with you and no one will hurt you. Many people in this city belong to me!" So Paul stayed in Corinth for a year and a half teaching God's Word. However, there were always Jews who challenged Paul and accused him of teaching people to worship God in ways that went against their Jewish laws.

When Paul left Corinth for Ephesus he took his new friends Aquila and Priscilla with him. There was a believer there named Apollos who knew the Scriptures very well and taught people with a lot of enthusiasm. However, Apollos didn't know the whole story about God's plan. He didn't know about John baptizing people before Jesus began His ministry. Aquila and Priscilla knew this information so they pulled Apollos aside and privately talked with him. They gave him the whole story of Jesus' work on Earth. Apollos was glad to get more information and he added that into his message as he continued teaching.

The Riot in Ephesus *Acts 19*

Paul's third missionary journey took him to Ephesus. "Did you receive the Holy Spirit when you believed?" he asked the believers there.

"No, we don't know what you're talking about," they said.

"Then what baptism did you experience?" he asked them.

"The baptism of John," they answered.

Paul explained that John's baptism was to show a desire to turn away from sin but that John encouraged people to

395

believe in Jesus. As soon as the people heard his explanations, they understood and were baptized in Jesus' name. When Paul placed his hands on them they received the Holy Spirit.

Then Paul went into the synagogue and began preaching. He stayed there for three months and preached about the kingdom of God. Some people rejected his message and said bad things about Paul's message to anyone who would listen. He left the synagogue and took the believers with him. He continued preaching in the lecture hall. He did that for two years so many people heard God's message.

God also gave Paul the power to do amazing miracles so many people were healed. A group of Jewish people were traveling from town to town casting out evil spirits. They tried to use Jesus' name to do their miracles saying, "I command you to come out in the name of Jesus whom Paul preaches about."

But one evil spirit said to them, "I know Jesus and I know Paul, but who are you?" Then the spirit jumped on them and attacked them. They ran out of the house to get away from it.

The news of this story spread quickly all through Ephesus. A great fear settled on the city and Jesus' name was greatly honored. Many people believed and confessed their sins.

Afterward Paul felt the Holy Spirit telling him to go to Macedonia. He went to several other cities too. But at the same time, trouble was brewing in Ephesus concerning the messages Paul had taught about the gospel. The trouble began with Demetrius, a silversmith who had a good business building silver shrines of the Greek goddess, Artemis. Demetrius called together all his workers and said, "You know our money comes from this business. You've heard about Paul who teaches that our gods are nothing. He's doing this in Ephesus and in other places too. Our goddess, Artemis, is losing respect because of Paul. She is being robbed of her importance!"

Demetrius's speech stirred up the crowd. They got more and more angry and rushed to the amphitheater where they thought they could capture Paul. His companions begged him not to go to the amphitheater. The crowd grew more and more rowdy until finally the mayor was able to get them quiet enough to listen to him. "Everyone knows that Ephesus is the guardian of the great Artemis. So don't do anything that will get you in trouble. If Demetrius has a case against Paul, then take it to court. But don't riot or the Roman government will come down on us!" So the crowd broke up.

Eutychus *Acts 20:7-12*

Paul and the group of men who traveled with him were in Troas. It was the first day of the week so they gathered with the believers there to celebrate the Lord's Supper. Paul preached and he had many things to tell the believers. He knew he was leaving the next day so he had to tell them everything in this one message. Paul preached and preached and soon it was midnight and he was still preaching. The group was meeting in an upstairs room with many little lamps lighting the room. One young man who was listening to Paul preach was sitting on the window sill. His name was Eutychus. He listened carefully to everything Paul said but as it got late he began to get sleepy. Finally, Eutychus fell asleep and when he did he fell right out of the window. He fell three stories down to the ground. Paul ran down the stairs to check on Eutychus and found that the fall had killed him. "Don't worry," Paul said to everyone around him, "he is alive!" Paul lifted Eutychus into his arms—and suddenly Eutychus was alive again! Everyone went back upstairs, ate the Lord's Supper, and Paul continued teaching them until the sun came up. Everyone was relieved that Eutychus was just fine.

Paul Is Arrested *Acts 21:17–22:29*

Paul said goodbye to the believers in Ephesus and headed for Jerusalem. Some of his friends begged him not to go there because the Jewish leaders were angry with him and had threatened to kill him. But Paul said that he was ready to die for the sake of Jesus. They couldn't convince him to change his mind so some of his friends went with him to Jerusalem. Paul met with the leaders of the church there and told them about his experiences preaching in other cities, and that many people were following Jesus now. They praised

God for all His work but then they said, "We know that a lot of Jews now believe in Jesus because of your preaching. However, we take the laws of Moses very seriously. The Christians here in Jerusalem tell us that you are teaching them to turn their backs on the laws of Moses. So now what can we do? Well, we have an idea. We have some men who are going to the temple to have their heads shaved and be a part of a purification cermony. Pay for them to have their heads shaved. Then everyone will know that the rumors are false and that you do

encourage people to obey the laws of Moses." Paul agreed to their plan and he went through the purification process the next day. But then some Jews from Asia saw him in the temple and started a riot against him. They grabbed him, yelling, "Help us! This is the man who teaches that people no longer have to obey Jewish laws! He even speaks against the temple!"

The whole city joined in the riot against Paul. He was dragged out of the temple and a great riot followed. They tried to kill him but word reached the Roman commander that the whole city was in a riot. He called out his soldiers and he ran through the crowd looking for Paul. When the people saw the commander coming, they stopped beating Paul. The commander arrested Paul and put chains on him. He asked the crowd who Paul was and what he had done. Some people shouted one thing and others shouted something else. He couldn't figure out what was going on. As they took Paul to prison the crowd followed behind shouting, "Kill him! Kill him!"

Paul asked permission to speak to the crowd and the commander let him. The crowd got very quiet when they saw Paul come forward to speak. Paul said, "I am a Jew and I have learned the Jewish laws and customs. I have obeyed them and am eager to honor God, just as you are. I persecuted those who followed Jesus. I even went to Damascus to stop them from preaching. But Jesus spoke to me while I was on that journey. I know now that He is God's Son. He told me that I have been chosen by God to take His message to the whole world. One day when I was in the temple I had a vision from God. He told me to leave Jerusalem because the people here would not believe my message. I argued with Him that you know me, you know my history. He still told me to leave Jerusalem. He told me to go far away and preach to the Gentiles."

When the crowd heard Paul say the world "Gentile" they went crazy and began shouting, "Kill him! Kill him!" The commander brought Paul inside and ordered that he be beaten. As the soldiers were beginning to beat him, Paul asked if it was legal to treat a Roman citizen in this way.

"You are a Roman citizen?" the commander asked.

"Yes I am. I am a citizen by birth," Paul said. So they untied him and did not beat him.

Paul Sails for Rome *Acts 22:30–27:12*

The commander freed Paul after learning that he was a Roman citizen. He had Paul come to a meeting of the High Council to find out what all the commotion was about. Paul addressed the council, "Brothers, I have always lived before God in a way that I can be proud of." Immediately the high priest commanded that those standing near Paul slap him on the mouth. "What are you doing?" Paul shouted. "You break the laws of God yourself by ordering me to be struck!" Others in the room criticized Paul for speaking that

way to the high priest but Paul didn't realize that it was the high priest who had spoken to him. He apologized and tried to continue. "I am a Pharisee my brothers. My whole family were Pharisees and I am on trial before you just because I now believe in the message of Jesus." The Pharisees on the council then began arguing with the Sadducees because their beliefs were so different. The argument got so strong that the commander removed Paul from the room.

That night the Lord spoke to Paul, "Don't be discouraged. You have told my message here in Jerusalem and I want you to continue preaching it in Rome."

The next morning a group of Jewish leaders got together and came up with a plan to kill Paul. They vowed that they would not eat or drink until he was dead. But Paul's nephew heard about their plan and he warned Paul of it. Paul had him speak to the commander and tell what he had heard. "Some of the Jews are going to ask you to bring Paul to the High Council tomorrow. Don't do it, though," the boy said. "A group of about 40 of them are going to ambush him and kill him." The commander listened to the boy and ordered that a group of 200 soldiers get ready to leave for Caesarea to take Paul to safety.

He sent Paul to Felix, the governor of Caesarea. The high priest followed Paul there and tried to bring charges against him but Felix put off the trial. Two years passed and Felix was succeeded by Festus. He heard the accusations against Paul but didn't know what to do so he sent Paul to King Agrippa. The king let Paul tell his side of the story and Paul clearly told him about Jesus' death and resurrection. During his speech, Paul asked to speak to Caesar in Rome. At the end of his message, Agrippa said, "I don't' see that this man has done anything wrong. He could have been set free if he hadn't asked to speak to Caesar."

So Paul was put on a boat to sail for Rome. There were several other prisoners on the boat too. The officers were very kind to Paul, even letting him get off the boat when it docked in various cities so he could visit with friends. Because of storms and other problems the trip took longer than expected and the season for safe sailing passed. Paul went to the ship's officers and said, "The season for safe travel is passed. If we go on we may have trouble, even a shipwreck." But the officer in charge didn't listen to them and they sailed once again.

Shipwreck! *Acts 27:13-44*

The boat sailed along, staying close to the shore but the weather suddenly changed and a powerful wind blew the ship out to sea. The sailors couldn't control where the ship went. Powerful winds battered the ship and the crew threw the cargo overboard to try to make the ship lighter so it wouldn't sink. The storm kept raging so they even threw equipment they needed overboard. The storm went on for several days and those on the ship were certain they were going to die. The men were too frightened and working too hard to even eat. Paul called the crew together and said, "Men, you should have listened to me. I told you this wasn't a safe time to travel. Anyway, don't worry. No one will die on this journey. An angel of God came to me last night and told me that we will arrive in Rome and I will have the chance to stand trial before Caesar. So don't be afraid. We're all going to be fine."

Around midnight on the 14th night of the storm the sailors saw land nearby.

They were afraid the ship would crash into the rocks near the land. They threw four anchors out but the ship continued to be blown toward the land. Finally they tried to get off the ship but Paul warned them that they would die if they got off in the powerful storm. So they stayed on board. "Please, eat something," Paul begged as morning came. They hadn't eaten anything for two weeks! "Eat and don't worry. I promise you that everyone will be safe!" Paul took some bread, thanked God for it, and passed it out to everyone on board.

The sailors tried to guide the ship between some of the rocks near the shore, but it crashed into the rocks and broke up. Some of the sailors wanted to kill the prisoners instead of letting them escape but the officer in command wouldn't allow that. He was protecting Paul. Everyone safely escaped the sinking ship and made it to shore.

They were on the island of Malta. The people of the island were very kind and built a fire for the men to warm themselves. Paul helped by gathering sticks and putting them on the fire. But as he was picking up sticks a poisonous snake wrapped itself around his hand. The people saw it hanging on him and thought it would kill him. "He must be a murderer and justice is prevailing. Since he didn't die at sea the snake will kill him," they said to one another. But Paul just shook the snake off of his hand and wasn't hurt at all. The people changed their minds and decided he must be a god.

It so happened that the father of the chief official on the island was very sick. Paul went in and prayed for the man and he was healed. Then all the other sick people on the island came and were cured by Paul's prayers to God too.

Three months after the shipwreck they sailed on to Rome. Even though he was a prisoner, Paul was allowed a private house to live in with a soldier to guard him. With the guard standing beside him he was allowed to preach there. For the next two years Paul lived there and preached about God's kingdom and no one tried to stop him.

Paul Writes Letters

Paul didn't waste any time. His goal of preaching and teaching about God's kingdom was always the first thing on his mind. Even when he was in prison he stayed focused on his goal. He wrote letters to the churches he had visited and to some that he had only heard about to encourage the believers in their faith. Many of the New Testament books are actually letters that Paul wrote. Romans was written to the church in Rome to share the good news of Jesus. The two Corinthians were written to the church in Corinth giving guidelines on how to live as believers. Galatians, Ephesians, Philippians, Colossians, and the two Thessalonians were also letters. The two letters to Timothy and one to Titus are also books of the New Testament. Paul was eager for believers to be strong in their faith and in their obedience to God.

The Revelation of John *The Book of Revelation*

J ohn was one of the 12 disciples of Jesus. He was arrested and sent to the island of Patmos. While John was there, God gave him a vision of what the future held. He wrote

about this vision to seven churches to warn them that the believers should be more obedient to God. He warned them about difficult times ahead and that they would have to suffer and be persecuted because they stood strong for Jesus. Some of the believers were being lazy about obeying God. Some were lazy about sharing the good news with others. Some could not get along with each other. John's letters warned them to be more serious about their faith.

God showed John the power and glory of Heaven in this vision. John shared in his letters the indescribable beauty and joy of Heaven. Jesus promised to come back to Earth and take believers with Him to Heaven. He promised to come soon.

Index of People and Places

A

Aaron, 97, 98, 100, 107, 113, 114, 118
Abednego, 208
Abel, 28, 29
Abigail, 157, 158
Abishai, 160, 167
Abraham (Abram), 41–63, 96, 121, 186, 248, 367
Absalom, 166–169
Adam, 23–28, 30, 138, 228
Adonijah, 169, 170
Ahab, 180, 184
Ahaz, 203
Ahithophel, 167
Ai, 44
Ananias, 370
Andrew, 255
Apollos, 394
Aquila, 393, 394
Aram, 194, 196
Ararat, 34, 35
Artaxerxes, 219
Artemis, 397
Asherah, 184, 186
Assyria, 203
Athens, 390, 391, 393

B

Baal, 184–186
Babel, 38, 40, 41
Babylon, 204, 207, 209
Barabbas, 334–336
Barak, 129, 131
Barnabas, 382, 383, 385
Bartholomew, 255

Bathsheba, 169
Belshazzar, 209, 210
Benjamin, 91, 92, 146
Berea, 390, 391
Bethany, 268, 303, 305
Bethel, 44, 187, 188
Bethlehem, 139, 150, 236-238, 240-242
Bethphage, 321
Bethuel, 63
Boaz, 139, 140

C

Caesar, 391, 404, 406
Caesarea, 376
Caiaphas, 330
Cain, 28–30
Caleb, 117
Cana, 256
Canaan, 41–43, 46, 63, 91, 92, 97, 100, 115, 117, 129-131
Capernaum, 296, 299
Corinth 393, 394
Cornelius, 376–378
Cyrene, 356

D

Damascus, 369, 370, 372, 373, 401
Daniel, 204–206, 210–212
Darius the Mede, 210–212
David, 140, 141, 150–152, 154–164, 166–170, 172, 174, 176, 178, 200, 203, 232, 235, 323, 364
Deborah, 129, 131, 132
Delilah, 136
Demetrius, 397

Mount Carmel, 184
Mount Nebo, 121
Mount of Olives, 326, 327
Mount Sinai, 96, 108, 110, 113, 114
Mount Tabor, 129

N

Naaman, 194, 195
Nabal, 157, 158
Nahor, 41
Naomi, 138-140
Nathan, 169, 170
Nazareth, 235, 242, 244, 246, 344,
    356
Neapolis, 386
Nebuchadnezzar, 207, 208, 210, 218
Nehemiah, 217, 219, 220
Nicodemus, 264, 265
Nile River, 93, 95, 108
Nineveh, 221, 223, 224
Noah, 30–35, 37, 38

O

Obadiah, 184
Obed, 140
Orpah, 139

P

Paddan-aram, 70
Paul (Saul), 368–373, 379,
    382, 383, 385–399, 401–404,
    407, 408
Peninnah, 141
Peter, 255, 282, 284, 311, 315–318,
    325, 329, 330, 332, 342,
    348–350, 356, 359, 360,
    375–381
Pharaoh, 43, 87–89, 93, 96–100,
    102–104

Philip, 255, 365–367
Philippi, 386
Philistines, 135-137, 147, 148, 151,
    152, 161, 162
Pilate, 333-336
Pool of Siloam, 292
Potiphar, 84–87
Priscilla, 393, 394
Promised land, 117, 120–122

R

Rachel, 73, 76, 77
Rahab, 122, 124, 126
Rebekah, 63, 64, 68
Red Sea, 102–105, 118, 122
Rehoboam, 178, 179
Rephidim, 108, 110
Reuben, 82, 83
Rhoda , 381
Rome, 356, 389, 402, 404, 406-408
Ruth, 138–140

S

Samaria, 194, 197, 266, 301, 352
Samothrace, 386
Samson, 135-137
Samuel, 141–144, 146–150, 163
Sarah (Sarai), 41, 43, 44, 49, 51,
    55-58
Saul (King), 141, 144, 146–149, 151,
    152, 154–156, 159–164
Saul (see Paul)
Sea of Tiberias, 348
Seir,   76
Seleucia, 382
Seth, 30
Shadrach, 208
Shaphan, 200, 201
Shechem, 80, 178